Benno Loewy

Correspondence Respecting the Enlistment of British

Subjects in the United States' Army

Benno Loewy

Correspondence Respecting the Enlistment of British Subjects in the United States' Army

ISBN/EAN: 9783337306960

Printed in Europe, USA, Canada, Australia, Japan

Cover: Foto ©Suzi / pixelio.de

More available books at **www.hansebooks.com**

NORTH AMERICA.
No. 17. (1864.)

CORRESPONDENCE

RESPECTING THE

ENLISTMENT

OF

BRITISH SUBJECTS

IN THE

UNITED STATES' ARMY.

Presented to the House of Commons by Command of Her Majesty.
1864.

LONDON:
PRINTED BY HARRISON AND SONS.
B

LIST OF PAPERS.

1.—"Copies of or Extracts from any Despatches from Her Majesty's Minister at Washington, relating to the Proceedings or Report of the Select Committee of the United States' Congress on Immigration, or to Bills upon that Subject brought into Congress: And also,

2.—"Copies or Extracts from Despatches or Reports respecting the Enlistment of Irish Immigrants at Boston and Portland in the Month of March last;

3.—"Or to the Enlistment of any of Her Majesty's Canadian Subjects in the United States Army."

1.—Despatches from Lord Lyons relating to the Proceedings or Report of the Select Committee of the United States' Congress on Immigration.

[No despatches on this subject have been received from Her Majesty's Minister at Washington.]

2.—Correspondence respecting the Enlistment of Irish Immigrants at Boston and Portland.

No. 1.

Consul Lousada to Earl Russell.—(Received March 4.)

My Lord,   Boston, March 15, 1864.

I HAVE the honour to inclose to your Lordship printed Report of the proceedings held by an indignation meeting in reference to the alleged kidnapping of a quantity of Irish labourers brought over to Portland in the steamer "Nova Scotian," by one Finney, ostensibly under pretext of obtaining them work and larger wages at the Cochetuate Waterworks, but in reality for the purpose of enlisting them, and obtaining the high bounties now offered. I was applied to on their behalf, but have not at present taken any action in the matter, as the meeting is a kind of Vigilance Committee, and will sift the affair thoroughly, but I reported details to Her Majesty's Minister at Washington, in case his Lordship wished to send me any instructions.

Mr. Kidder, the merchant who is implicated in this transaction, also called on me yesterday, and stated that he meant to have employed them as labourers only. With the information I had in my possession as to the real nature of the scheme, I confined myself to simply hearing what he chose to tell me. I am informed that Finney is a person of bad reputation, and that the documents he produced in Ireland in defence of his course were not genuine. This, however, will be elicited, and I shall send the Report of the adjourned meeting as soon as it takes place.

I understand from some of the men, who also have been to my office, that many more deluded Irish are on their road, similarly entrapped, although Mr. Kidder positively denied being cognizant of the fact; and I hope that I am misinformed thereon.

The bounties both of the United States and of the several States, added to local premiums, amount to 700 dollars, and even 820 dollars, besides 15 to 25 to the bringer in of a recruit, and as the poor Irish are generally made drunk, and given at the outside 25 dollars, the sharks who prey on them collect the balance, and thus a cargo of 120, as in this instance, would net a very large profit to the speculators.

There are some features in these transactions which involuntarily recall to my mind my experiences in Cuba; I trust, however, that the publication of what those who hire themselves as labourers may expect on this side will check the traffic.

I have, &c.

(Signed)   F. LOUSADA.

P.S.—Subsequently to writing this, the "Courier" publishes "a card" from Mr. Kidder, copies of which I also inclose.

F. L.

Inclosure 1 in No. 1.

Newspaper Extract.

OUTRAGEOUS IMPOSITION. ONE HUNDRED DUBLIN YOUNG MEN ENTICED TO THIS COUNTRY ON FALSE PRETENCES.—The Irish citizens of Charlestown and Boston have been greatly excited this week, in consequence of the arrival in Charlestown of eighty-six young Irishmen from the city of Dublin, under extraordinary circumstances. These young men, 102 in all, left Liverpool on February 27th, in a steamer for Portland, which reached that city on Wednesday morning, March 9th. The men took an early breakfast and then landed. A few of them strayed away from their companions, but the remainder came on to Boston in the afternoon train, in charge of the Emigrant agent, a Mr. Finney, under whose inducements and promises they left their home. Upon their arrival in this city, the men were conducted to an old building on Bunker Hill-street, Charlestown, belonging to Mr. Jerome G. Kidder, of this city, formerly used for his business purposes, but now improved as a " Mission House." At this building nothing was provided for the reception of the men ; no food, although they had eaten nothing since early morning and it was now half-past 9 o'clock ; no bedding, no comforts of any kind, not even straw to sleep upon. After a little while, some crackers and cheese were procured, and a tub of ale was brought in with which the wearied men sought to refresh themselves. In the morning they had whisky for breakfast, and a number of those who partook of it were made senseless.

Mr. Kidder, the owner of the building, presented himself on the night of their arrival, and told the men, so it is reported by several of them, that the work they were brought over to do was not ready; but that need not make no difference, they need not be idle a single day ; they could enlist at once, and recommended the 28th, an Irish regiment, to them. Upon this, the suspicions were confirmed which had been growing upon the men, that they had been deceived and enticed from their homes upon false pretences.

The men are fine, stalwart fellows, young mechanics, all from the city of Dublin. One of them, a young man by the name of Ward, is a comedian, who has acted upon the Dublin boards and in the Irish Provinces, in parts like those assumed by Barney Williams and Florence. Their story is, that they were induced to come to this country through the representation of this Mr. Finney, who was announced in the papers as an " emigration agent for the principal railroads in New England, who was commissioned to procure 1,000 labourers." The terms he offered them were a free passage, work immediately upon arrival, a new suit of clothes, and 2*l*. a month and found, for wages. Mr. Finney now declares himself to be agent for Mr. Kidder, and Mr. Kidder protests that he caused the men to be brought over here in good faith, actually and *bonâ fide* to work upon the Charlestown waterworks, and that he was ready on Friday to take as many of the men to West Medford as would consent to go, and put them at once to work. He says, moreover, that he has no knowledge of who ordered the liquor to the men on the night of their arrival. It was certainly done without his privity.

The condition of the men the morning after their arrival in Charlestown was anything but gratifying. Their number had already been diminished by those left behind at Portland, and of these, the recruiting agents had snapped up eight. Without money, without friends, with scanty clothing, with no means to procure sustenance, they would have suffered greatly, had not kind-hearted countrywomen supplied their wants. Recruiting agents hovered round them, and in the course of the day gobbled up several. On the evening of Thursday they had another interview with Mr. Kidder, when they were told the hall must be cleared, and they would not have had a place to lay their heads had not Captain John Warren, who keeps an establishment on that street, near by, bestirred himself and procured billets for them upon the neighbours round. Yesterday morning they were still in Bunker Hill-street, subsisting upon charity, and still pestered with recruiting agents. In the course of the forenoon Mr. Kidder again appeared among them, offering to take as many as would go to the waterworks at West Medford. But the men had lost confidence in him. They cost Mr. Kidder 70 dollars a head to land them in Boston. It will prove a poor speculation as it has turned out. But if they had taken his recommendation on the night of their arrival, to enlist, he might have made himself whole and something more.

The Irish citizens of Boston and vicinity, feeling indignant at the imposition practised upon their countrymen, called a meeting at the Stackpole House to investigate the facts in the case, which was very largely attended. Charles F. Donnelly, Esq., was called to the chair, and Edward Ryan was appointed Secretary. The Chairman, in stating the objects of the meeting, recited the circumstances under which the men came here, as stated in the first part of this article. From the facts as they had been presented to him, he believed that the original intent of parties who brought the men over was to make them part of the quota of Massachusetts. The men themselves think they have been duped, and that it was the intention to sell them to the military service.

Martin Mc Manus, an employé on the Midland and Great Western Railway, one of the emigrants, said to the meeting:—He had full employment at 2s. 10d. a-day, and that he was induced by the representations of Mr. Finney—free passage, steady work, 2l. British a-month and board, and two suits of clothes a-year—to come over. He had found no work. He was not told by Finney where the work would be, but that he should be treated of the best. Was told on board the ship a party would meet them on the wharf in Portland—a real gentleman and a good friend, who would take care of them, and they must take off their hats and give him three cheers. Their supper, when they arrived in Bunker Hill Street, after fasting all day, consisted of a barrel of crackers and a cheese, with a knife on it, and the question was, "Who shall?" and there was a scramble, some getting enough for five, others getting nothing. For breakfast they had buckets of whiskey. That night, without beds, or even straw, enlisting agents were among them all the time. Finney also staid with them. They said the waterworks were done up, and the only thing for them to do was to enlist. Mr. Kidder, himself, told them he could find different men to take them ; but if they were inclined to enlist, they had better do it, for he had no work for them to do.

John Glannan, labourer of Dublin, who earned 3s. a-day four or five days in the week, was induced to come on similar representations as Mc Manus had spoken of. Finney would give them nothing at Portland, and at the hall in Charlestown a policeman was stationed on the first night to prevent their going out. Mr. Kidder told them he had work for thirty or forty, but no more, on the waterworks at 1 dollar 25 cents a-day.

Others made statements of a like character.

P. R. Sullivan, a friend to Mr. Kidder, expressed his belief that Mr. K. had acted from good motives. Mr. Kidder had written to Finney not to ship any men of the 22nd of February, but they were shipped on the 25th of February, and came unexpectedly. Under the circumstances he had done the best he could. He was not prepared with work for the men, but told them if they thought fit to enlist he should claim 70 dollars from each to reimburse expenses.

E. Smythe, Representative from Ward 1, Boston, asked if the men were intended for waterworks why their shipment was suspended just at the season was approaching when such work could be prosecuted? What could men do in digging and tearing up the earth in February? If Mr. Kidder had told his agent not to send more men till later in the season there would have been sense in it. He believed that it was intended to have the men here just prior to a certain epoch which all were looking for—the draft, and they would come very handy then.

Mr. Martin Lynch said he had heard at Concord, N. H., long before these men arrived, that this same emigration agent, Mr. Finney, had been engaged last summer in bringing substitutes to New Hampshire and selling them. He became notorious as a substitute broker, and made money by it. After he was arrested in Dublin on suspicion of employing men to make soldiers of them, he wrote that he would make 30,000 dollars out of the operation he was then engaged in—engaging men to work on railroads, but really to make substitutes of them. Now, asked Mr. Ryan, if Mr. Kidder was honest in getting these men here, would he select such a person as Finney for his agent?

A Voice.—The man who sent Finney was worse than Finney himself.

Mr. Lynch.—What we want, gentlemen, is to sift this matter to the bottom, find who the guilty persons are and punish them. He concluded by moving that a committee be appointed by the chair to investigate all the facts in the case to report at a future meeting. Adopted.

Mr. Edward Ryan offered some remarks to the effect that Mr. Kidder ought not to be judged and condemned without a hearing. The meeting had heard one side ; let the other side have a hearing. It might be that after all Mr. Kidder had done nothing worthy of censure.

The Chairman named as the Committee, Eneas Smythe, Dr. Bath Morris, James Dowling, Edward Ryan, Martin Lynch, Charles F. Donnelly, John Horan, and Michael McCaffrey.

The same gentlemen, with the addition of P. R. Sullivan, were appointed a committee to collect subscriptions for the relief of the immigrants. A subscription list was opened and upwards of 50 dollars was subscribed on the spot.

A Mr. Shea, one of the emigrants who had just entered the meeting, said he went to the waterworks at West Medford that afternoon, and was introduced to the contractor, Mr. McDonald. That gentleman said that he had never had anything to do with getting men from Ireland to work. Knew nothing about these emigrants until yesterday, when Mr. Kidder came to him and said he had the men here, but seeing how matters had turned he could make no good of them. Mr. McDonald employed twenty-three of the emigrants. He expressed the belief that Mr. Kidder had got the men over here for the purpose of enlisting them.

The Investigation Committee will meet this forenoon at 11 o'clock, at the Stackpole House, when Mr. Kidder and Mr. Finney and their friends are invited to be present.

The meeting stands adjourned to a week from Monday next, at the Hall of the Constitutional Democratic Club, to hear the report of investigation.

Messrs. Lynch, Donnelly and Ryan are a Committee to disburse the funds for relief to the destitute emigrants.

Inclosure 2 in No. 1.

Newspaper Extract.

WE print, on the outside of to-day's "Courier," a card of Mr. J. G. Kidder, according to his request. We prefer to make no remarks upon the subject until the investigation which is in progress is concluded. In connection with this subject, however, we quote the following from the Dublin "Freeman's Journal:"—

"SUSPICIOUS.—On Tuesday evening, 23rd of February, fifty-six young men left the North Wall by the steamer 'St. Columba' for Liverpool, en route for Boston, United States. The emigrants were engaged by an agent here from America as workmen on a line of railway now said to be in course of construction. By the conditions of the agreement the emigrants cannot work save at the railway; but it is stated that they will be granted permission to join the Federal army. They will be inspected at Liverpool prior to embarking in a ship chartered to take 700 Irishmen to America."

"A Card.

"The morning papers of Saturday contain an account of a meeting of Irish citizens, in which I am charged with inhumanity in the treatment of some emigrants from Ireland, whose passage I had become responsible for.

"This was an experiment to see if by possibility a plan of importing labourers could be made self-sustaining.

"The depths of poverty from which this 100 men have been taken may be inferred from the fact that before they were shipped they all signed an agreement to work for one year for 10 dollars per month and their board and lodging, the cost of their passage to be deducted from their first earnings. Owing to the want of notice of the arrival of the men at Portland (they arriving here at 9 o'clock P.M.) it was impossible to find beds for them, and they were placed in a new commodious building in Charlestown, furnished with settees and warmed and lighted. An ample supply of such refreshments as could be got at that late hour was furnished, there being no time to have meat cooked. On the following morning a breakfast of eggs, bread, tea, and what cooked provisions (hams, roast and boiled beef) the Parker House could supply, which was ample in quantity and the quality which had been provided for the guests of the Parker House.

"By very great exertions I was able, through the kindness of Messrs. Stephenson, engineer, and McDonald, contractor, aided by the directors of the Charlestown Water Works, to make arrangements that the men should be taken on to work at once at the going rate of wages.

"My object being philanthropic to aid these poor men, as well as to supply the great need we have of labour here, I told the men that by their agreement they were bound to work for 10 dollars per month for a year, but that I had determined that I would give in to them all of the difference between that price and the rate which the water contractors would give, which was 1 dollar 50 cents per day.

"That they should have all of their first earnings to furnish themselves with clothing, and that after this their earnings must be applied to reimburse me for what I paid for each of their passages, according to their agreement; and that so soon as that was made good, all that they earned would belong to themselves, thus really giving to them what might be equal to 120 or 150 dollars in the year more than they expected.

"I proposed that 30 of them should go by the 2·30 train that day, but when the time arrived what remained of them refused to go. In the evening, ample provision having been made of food and beds, they again promised to go out on the 7·10 train. I sent a man to take them to the depôt, but they again refused.

"On the 2·30 train I finally succeeded in getting off 15, and Mr. McDonald writes to me that he has 25, and can take up to 100.

"The only hardship, if it is a hardship, that these men have undergone is that of having to sleep for one night in a comfortable room on settees or on the floor, and which, from the circumstances of the case, was unavoidable.

"I understand that at the meeting of Irish citizens, some 50 dollars were subscribed to aid the men. It was, I think, quite unnecessary to do this. If, instead of it, they had insisted with the men that they should go to work, it would have been much better for them. I do not hear that anything was said or done at the meeting relative to the forfeiture of their agreement by those men who have run away, or that any steps were taken to make up the loss to me of the cost of their passages, of which I am to be defrauded.

"The conduct of the men on this occasion will no doubt preclude the probability of any further attempts of the kind being made, although I am informed from the best authority that 10,000 men could be engaged on the same terms as these.

"I would give notice that any of the men who are willing to go to work have only to proceed to West Medford, from the Lowell Railroad depôt, and inquire of the conductors, who will direct them to the waterworks.

"The papers who have given circulation to the account of the meeting mentioned above will confer a favour by publishing this statement.

(Signed) "J. G. KIDDER."

No. 2.

Lord Lyons to Earl Russell.—(Received March 29.)

My Lord,   Washington, March 14, 1864.

I HAVE the honour to inclose a copy of a despatch from Her Majesty's Consul at Boston, informing me of practices which have been resorted to in order to entrap into enlisting into the United States' army a large number of Irishmen brought to this country by a man named Finney, who is stated to have been not long ago arrested in Ireland on the charge of being engaged in recruiting there for the Federal service.

I inclose also a copy of the answer which I have made to the Consul's despatch.

I have, &c.
(Signed)   LYONS.

Inclosure 1 in No. 2.

Consul Lousada to Lord Lyons.

My Lord,   Boston, March 11, 1864.

I HAVE the honour to lay before your Lordship the outline of a deposition just made before me by a respectable householder, Martyn Lynch, proprietor of the "Stackpole Hotel," Boston. It is to the effect that one Finney, a man lately arrested in Ireland for recruiting, but who got off under the plea that he was obtaining labourers for the public works at Charleston, Massachusetts, brought over 120 Irishmen to Portland by last steamer, and had conveyed them thence to Charlestown, adjoining and part of; and having located them in some hall, afterwards took in four gallons of whiskey, got several of them to enlist and secured the money. The hall in question is owned by one Kidder, of State-street, who is either partner with Finney, or, probably, his employer. A Mr. Warren, a grocer residing in Charleston, interfered and spoilt the plot a little by telling these men how shamefully they had been imposed upon; but subsequently more whiskey was introduced, and Martyn Lynch supposes that by this time they are all secured.

The bounties now approaching 700 dollars, the speculators must clear about 500 dollars a-man. An indignation meeting of Irish is to be held this evening at the "Stackpole House," as many more victims are on the road, and some prompt action is desirable. This is the substance of the testimony of Mr. Lynch, and he has promised me further details to-morrow.

I report this briefly to save to-day's post, in case your Lordship should desire to send me any instructions hereon.

I have, &c.
(Signed)   F. LOUSADA.

Inclosure 2 in No. 2.

Lord Lyons to Consul Lousada.

Sir,   *Washington, March* 13, 1864.

I HAVE received this morning your despatch of the day before yesterday, giving the outline of a deposition made before you respecting improper means which appear to have been employed to induce a large number of Irishmen, who have recently landed in this country, to enlist in the United States' army.

In the absence of more detailed information, I can do little more than instruct you to use every means to obtain such evidence of the practices of which these British subjects appear to have been the victims as shall enable me to bring their cases before the United States' Government, with some hope of obtaining their discharge.

It would also be desirable that you should lose no time in obtaining a list of the names of the individuals enlisted, and such information concerning each of them as may be useful in tracing him.

If you have any hope of being able, by application to the local authorities, military or civil, to obtain the release of these British subjects at once, or the punishment of the men by whom they have been deceived, you will of course take immediate steps for the purpose.

You will in any case send me speedy and full information on the whole matter, with a view to such representations as it may be proper for me to make to the Central Government here.

I am, &c.
(Signed)   LYONS.

No. 3.

Earl Russell to Lord Lyons.

My Lord,   *Foreign Office, March* 31, 1864.

I HAVE received your despatch of the 14th instant and its inclosures, respecting the proceedings of the man Pheeny or Finney to induce the Irishmen who accompanied him to America to enlist in the United States' Army; and I have to instruct you to bring these proceedings to the notice of Mr. Seward, and to request that he will cause an inquiry to be made respecting them.

I am, &c.
(Signed)   RUSSELL.

No. 4.

Lord Lyons to Earl Russell.—(Received April 3.)

My Lord,   *Washington, March* 22, 1864.

WITH reference to my despatch of the 14th instant, I have the honour to transmit to your Lordship copies of two further despatches from Mr. Consul Lousada respecting the means employed at a place near Boston for the purpose of enlisting in the United States' army a large number of immigrants, who appear to have been brought to this country by a man named Finney on board the steamer " Nova Scotian."

Her Majesty's Consul at Portland informs me that he had sent to your Lordship a copy of a despatch which he wrote to me on the 17th instant, and from which I learned that still more unjustifiable practices had been used to induce seven Irishmen belonging to the same party to enlist at Portland. I have the honour to transmit to your Lordship herewith further papers relative to this affair.

Among the papers your Lordship will find a copy of note, in which I have stated to Mr. Seward that if it be not thought proper to discharge these seven men at once, I trust that a serious inquiry into the circumstances under which their enlistment took place will be made, and that measures will be immediately taken to prevent their being forwarded to the army, or placed in actual service, pending the investigation.

I have in the same note directed to Mr. Seward's attention to the case of the Irishmen enlisted at Boston, and have addressed to him an earnest request, not only that prompt redress may be given for the wrongs suffered by the individuals whose cases I have brought before him, but that measures may be taken effectually to protect in future British subjects arriving in the United States from the practices of unscrupulous recruiting agents.

I have, &c.
(Signed)   LYONS.

Inclosure 1 in No. 4.

Consul Lousada to Lord Lyons.

My Lord,   *Boston, March* 12, 1864.
I HAVE the honour to inclose an extract from the Boston "Courier" of to-day, containing an account of the meeting held yesterday evening in reference to those Irishmen brought over by Finney (or Phinney), and subject of my despatch of the 11th instant.
                                                        I have, &c.
                                            (Signed)   F. LOUSADA.

Inclosure 2 in No. 4.

Newspaper Extract.

[See Inclosure 1 in No. 1.]

Inclosure 3 in No. 4.

Consul Lousada to Lord Lyons.

My Lord,   *Boston, March* 17, 1864.
IN reference to my despatch of the 12th instant, I inclose a copy of a "card" published by Mr. Kidder, which, as the "Courier" justly observes, can be taken *quantum valeat.* I am in train to get an authentic list of the men brought over, and hope to forward it to-morrow. Meanwhile the "Indignation Committee" are hard at work, and some curious developments are promised for the next meeting, a report of which is to be published and will be duly forwarded.
                                                        I have, &c.
                                            (Signed)   F. LOUSADA.

Inclosure 4 in No. 4.

Newspaper Extract.

[See Inclosure 2 in No. 1.]

Inclosure 5 in No. 4.

Thomas Tulley and six others to Lord Lyons.

My Lord,   *Philadelphia, March* , 1864.
SINCE writing the inclosed, we have been sent to the seat of war, and we will be in Washington to-morrow. Will your Lordship have us justified and released? I believe we are going to Alexandria. Don't forget your Lordship's obedient servants.
                                            (Signed)   T. TULLEY.

Inclosure 6 in No. 4.

Thomas Tulley and six others to Lord Lyons.

My Lord,   *Camp Berry, Portland, America, March* 13, 1864.
I BEG leave most respectfully to intimate to you that I sailed from Liverpool on the 25th February, 1864, for the purpose of making good my position in life. I and my companions, whose names are attached hereto, arrived in Portland on the 9th of March instant. We landed with tickets in our possession to bring us to Boston, but scarcely were we in America six hours, when we were arrested, put into prison, where we remained until the morning following, when we made application to have ourselves released; this was denied us, unless we became American soldiers. This we individually declined, and after being imprisoned for upwards of thirty hours, without a drink or a mouthful of food, we were obliged to go the recruiting depôt in Portland, and become soldiers, solely on account of thirst and hunger, together with the hopes that were held out to us by the Deputy-Governor of the prison and his recruiting myrmidons. We had not even an opportunity of making our case known to the English Consul, but when the opportunity offered Mr. Murray called on us, and signified his disapprobation. Notwithstanding, I fear we will be compelled to proceed into the American army towards the Potomac. Now, my Lord, I most respectfully submit that it is contrary to the rules of civilization to have subjects of Her Britannic Majesty sold as a lot of slaves, and therefore we appeal to your Lordship for justice. We are enrolled in the 20th Maine Infantry Regiment,

C

and the British Consul was here last evening, and told us he would do his utmost for us, and that if he did not succeed he would write to your Lordship. We are about representing the matter to the Secretary of State in England, but previous to our doing so, we submit our case to your Lordship, fully hoping that you will not tolerate British subjects being kidnapped after six hours' residence in America.

Your Lordship no doubt will know the proper source to apply to for our liberation.

(Signed) THOMAS TULLEY.
EDWD. CASSIDY.
JAMES HIGGINS.
M. F. BYRNE.
MARTIN HOGAN.
THOMAS BURKE.
MICHAEL MORAN.

Inclosure 7 in No. 4.

Lord Lyons to Consul Murray.

Sir, *Washington, March* 18, 1864.

I TRANSMIT to you copies of two letters which I have received this morning, and from which it would appear that seven British subjects, Thomas Tulley, Edward Cassidy, James Higgins, Michael F. Byrne, Martin Hogan, Thomas Burke, Michael Moran, were arrested on landing at Portland, and have been forced into the United States' military service.

It seems that these men were in communication with you when they were at Portland, and I have to request you to make to me a full report on the case, in order that I may be able to determine whether it will be proper for me to take measures to obtain their discharge.

I am, &c.
(Signed) LYONS.

Inclosure 8 in No. 4.

Lord Lyons to Mr. Seward.

Sir, *Washington, March* 19, 1864.

I BEG you to take into immediate consideration the despatch from Her Majesty's Consul at Portland,* and its inclosures, copies of which I do myself the honour to submit to you herewith.

They recount the circumstances under which, according to the statements made to the Consul, seven Irishmen, British subjects, who landed at Portland on the 9th of this month, have been enlisted in the United States' army. At the request of the Consul, Acting Assistant Provost-Marshal General for the State of Maine, Major Gardiner, sent an order to detain these men at Portland, until an investigation could be made; but before the arrival of the order the men had been sent off to join the 20th regiment of Maine Volunteers, now stationed with the army of the Potomac. I myself received yesterday a letter from them written at Philadelphia on their way to Washington; and I conclude that they must now have reached this place.

If it be not thought proper to order the men to be discharged at once, I trust that a serious inquiry into the circumstances under which their enlistment took place will be made, and that measures will be immediately taken to prevent their being forwarded to the army or placed in actual service pending the investigation.

The names of the men are,—1. Thomas Tulley; 2. Michael Byrne; 3. James Higgins; 4. Edward Cassidy; 5. Thomas Burke; 6. Michael Moran; 7. Martin Hogan.

I beg you to be so good as to let me know where these men now are.

It seems proper that I should also mention to you that it is reported to me by Her Majesty's Consul at Boston that a large number of Irishmen brought over by the same packet and in charge of the same person, a man named Finney, have been practised on in a not unsimilar manner in the neighbourhood of that city, and enlisted in the United States' army. It will probably be my duty to address you again on this subject, when I receive more complete information from the Consul.

* Inclosure 1 in No. 5.

I cannot conclude without an earnest request that, not only prompt redress may be given for such wrongs as may have been endured by the individuals whose cases I have now brought to your notice, but that measures may be taken effectually to protect in future British subjects arriving in the United States from the practices of unscrupulous recruiting agents.

I have, &c.
(Signed)   LYONS.

Inclosure 9 in No. 4.

Lord Lyons to Consul Murray.

Sir,   *Washington, March 19, 1864.*

WITH reference to my despatch of yesterday I have to inform you that I have received this morning your despatch of the day before yesterday's date, relative to the enlistment into the United States' army of Thomas Tulley and six other Irish emigrants.

I have transmitted copies of your despatch and of its inclosures to the Secretary of State of the United States, with a note requesting that if it be not thought proper to discharge these men at once, a serious inquiry into the circumstances under which they were enlisted may be made, and measures be taken immediately to prevent their being forwarded to the army or placed in actual service pending the investigation.

I have also spoken to the Secretary of State about the case, and pressed him to take steps concerning it without delay.

I am, &c.
(Signed)   LYONS.

No. 5.

Consul Murray to Earl Russell.—(Received April 4.)

My Lord,   *Portland, March 19, 1864.*

I HAVE the honour to transmit herewith a copy of a despatch, together with its inclosures, that I addressed to Her Majesty's Minister at Washington on the 17th instant on the subject of the complaint of seven Irishmen who arrived at Portland on the 9th instant on board the steam-ship "Nova Scotian," and who state that they were entrapped into the military service of the United States.

I have, &c.
(Signed)   HENRY JOHN MURRAY.

Inclosure 1 in No. 5.

Consul Murray to Lord Lyons.

My Lord,   *Portland, March 17, 1864.*

I HAVE the honour to transmit herewith copies of a correspondence I have had with the Acting Assistant Provost Marshal General for this State, Major Gardiner, and with the Mayor of Portland, upon the subject of the improper enlistment of seven Irishmen, British subjects, who arrived at Portland on the 9th instant on board of the steam-ship "Nova Scotian," under a contract, entered into in Ireland, to proceed to Boston to be employed there, but who were enticed into a liquor-store on their immediate arrival, made drunk, and were put into confinement in consequence of a breach of the peace, and while there, they state, they were forced and intimidated to enter the military service of the United States.

In reply to my request, Major Gardiner gave orders for the men to be detained until an investigation was made, but it appears that they were sent away from Camp Berry, previous to the arrival of the order, to join the 20th Regiment of Maine Volunteers, now stationed with the Army of the Potomac.

From the Mayor I have as yet received no reply.

I have, &c.
(Signed)   HENRY JOHN MURRAY.

C 2

Inclosure 2 in No. 5.

Thomas Tulley and six others to Consul Murray.

Sir,   *Camp Berry, Portland, March* 11, 1864.

WE, the Undersigned, beg leave most respectfully to bring to your notice the fact that we were brought out from Ireland by a person of the name of Finney, for the purpose of working in Boston. We arrived in Portland on the 9th instant, but having lost the train which was to convey us with the remainder of the party we came with, we were put into prison and could not gain our liberation or food unless we submitted to enrol ourselves in the American service, which we ultimately did through mere compulsion and privation. We are now in the camp, and about being forwarded to the interior, and therefore as British subjects we claim that protection which is granted to the people of that country throughout the globe. Will you therefore, Sir, as Consul of our country, inquire into the matter at once, and gain for us our liberty, as it is a most crying shame to see British subjects treated in the manner we have been. Should you not interfere in the matter will you kindly say so, that we may represent the matter to the Secretary of State in London, as most decidedly no country can stand by such conduct. The police first confines us; keeps us in prison and refuses to give us our liberty or food until we enlist. Although we had our passage certificates to Boston in our possession we were not even six hours in America before we were entrapped.

Hoping for you kind consideration, we are, &c.

(Signed)   THOMAS TULLEY.
                          MICHL. BYRNE.
                          JAMES HIGGINS.
                          EDWD. CASSIDY.
                          THOS. BURKE.
                          MICHAEL MORAN.
                          MARTIN HOGAN.

Inclosure 3 in No. 5.

Consul Murray to Major Gardner.

Sir,   *Portland, March* 14, 1864.

I BEG to forward you herewith a copy of a letter I have received, signed by seven Irishmen, British subjects, who arrived in this city on Wednesday last by the steam-ship "Nova Scotian," and who complained that they have been entrapped and intimidated into the service of the United States. At a personal interview I had with these men yesterday at Camp Berry (through the kindness of Lieutenant-Colonel Merrill) they assured me in the most positive manner that their statements were perfectly true, and declared many things to me that tend to prove a systematic attempt was successfully made by the brokers, and connived at by the police, to get them into such a position that would force them to enlist.

The wise provisions of the paragraph No. 926 regarding the duties of recruiting officers appear to have been wantonly disregarded, and men who came out to this country under a contract that was binding upon their parts, to serve in industrial operations at Boston and elsewhere, have been forced to enter the military service of the United States.

May I request, on the part of these men, that an official examination may be made into their respective cases, and that they be detained at Camp Berry until the validity of their enlistment be proved?

I have, &c.

(Signed)   HENRY JOHN MURRAY

Inclosure 4 in No. 5.

Revised Regulations for the Army.

DUTIES OF RECRUITING OFFICERS.

THEY will not allow any man to be deceived or inveigled into the service by false representations, but will in person explain the nature of the service, the length of the term, the pay, clothing, rations, and other allowances to which a soldier is entitled by law, to every man before he signs the enlistment.

Inclosure 5 in No. 5.

Consul Murray to the Mayor of Portland.

Sir,   *Portland, March* 14, 1864.

I HAVE received a representation from seven Irishmen, British subjects, to the effect that they arrived at Portland on Wednesday last on board of the steam-ship " Nova Scotian." That they had signed a contract in Ireland with a person named Finney, binding themselves to work at Boston for a certain monthly stipend and their board; and they arrived here with the intention of proceeding to Boston in the railway with their companions, but that on their landing early in the morning, without having breakfasted, they were immediately conducted to a neighbouring liquor store, and there treated to liquor so that the greater part of them got drunk and knew not what they did, and shortly afterwards found themselves locked up at the police office, in the new City Government House. That they were kept without food or drink, although they repeatedly asked for both. That while there enlisting brokers were admitted to them, and who told them that they would be subjected to sixty days' imprisonment which they would avoid by enlisting. They refused to enlist, and were then told that they would have no food until they did enlist. Upon this they signed the enlistment papers, and were taken before the Provost-Marshal, but on their then refusing to enter the service they were returned to confinement. This happened two or three times, and fearing that they would be starved, they at last agreed to enlist. The town bounty of 200 dollars was then placed in their hands, and they were provided with a good dinner, but still kept locked up. They state that shortly after the receipt of the bounty money, soldiers, or persons in the uniform of the United States, were admitted to them, who palmed off upon them silver watches and jewellery, almost forcing them to buy them. I went to the camp yesterday, and had a long interview with these men, who declared most solemnly to the truth of their foregoing statement.

I therefore deem it my duty to lay these circumstances before you, feeling assured that it can never be the intention of the United States' Government that persons coming over to this country, under a special contract, should be inveigled and intimidated into their military service.

There can be but little doubt that these men were systematically treated to liquor on their immediate arrival at Portland by the agents of the Recruiting Brokers, who well knew that the results of their intemperance would lead the men to the police office, where they could be acted upon with the connivance of the police.

I see by the public papers that a " Foreign Immigration Society " has been formed for this State of Maine. I need hardly remark that when the treatment of this batch of contract emigrants, both at Portland and at Boston, becomes publicly known in Europe, it must seriously affect the success of the association, for few respectable hardworking people would like to come out to a country where within a few hours after their arrival they find themselves forced to enter the military service of that country, instead of following the peaceful avocations they had contracted for.

May I request, therefore, that you will be pleased to inquire into the truth of these statements, and I would express a hope that care may be taken on the arrival of vessels conveying British emigrants, to put a stop to designing and cruel proceedings which the Government of the United States would be the first to repudiate.

I have, &c.

(Signed)   HENRY JOHN MURRAY.

Inclosure 6 in No. 5.

Major Gardiner to Consul Murray.

Office of Acting Assistant Provost Marshal General,
Sir, *Augusta, Maine, March 15, 1864.*
YOUR letter of the 14th in relation to certain men claiming to have been improperly enlisted is just arrived.

I write by mail to-day to the officer commanding the Camp at Portland, requesting him to detain these men until an investigation can be made.

Very respectfully,
(Signed) J. W. T. GARDINER.

No. 6.

Consul Lousada to Earl Russell.—(Received April 4.)

My Lord, *Boston, March 21, 1864.*
IN continuation of the case of the Irishmen brought over to this country by Finney (subject of my despatch of the 15th instant), I now have the honour to inclose a leading article of to-day's " Courier," which logically confutes the sophistry of Mr. Kidder's " Card," and will repay perusal, as really setting forth the true nature of the transaction. The final action of the Committee is postponed until Friday, and I shall be able by the subsequent mail to report the result.

I have, &c.
(Signed) F. LOUSADA.

Inclosure in No. 6.

Extract from the " Courier."

THE IRISH EMIGRATION ENLISTMENT SCHEME. A SUBSTITUTE BROKER'S SPECULATION FRUSTRATED.—The Committee appointed at the Stackpole House meeting, to investigate facts connected with the arrival of 102 young men from Dublin, in charge of Mr. Finney, their contract with him before leaving their home, and the treatment they received upon their arrival in this country and immediately subsequent thereto, have been diligently and conscientiously pursuing the duties assigned them, and will be ready to report at the adjourned meeting to be held on Friday evening in the hall of the Constitutional Democratic Club. The Committee have held meetings almost daily; they have examined quite a number of the emigrants: Mr. Jerome G. Kidder was before the Committee three hours at one of the sessions, and Mr. Finney, the agent, has also been present. The meetings have been conducted without bias, and all persons who had anything pertinent to the investigation to offer have been invited to speak, and have been listened to patiently and attentively. Without presuming to anticipate the report of the Committee, we desire to call attention to one or two prominent features in the transactions that have been disclosed during this inquiry.

It is made very evident by the testimony that has been taken, that the shipment of the 102 men whose particular case is under consideration, was part of a widely-extended, ramified scheme, in which more than Mr. Kidder and Mr. Finney are involved, and the outlines of which, at least, were known and approved in high official quarters before it had been tried, experimentally—before, in fact, Finney had sailed from this country. The objections to this scheme do not arise because its prime object was to procure recruits for the armies, but because it appears a scheme of fraud and false pretence upon the emigrant, and of violation to the foreign enlistment laws of another country, calculated to bring discredit upon all who connive at it, and add to difficulties which are already aggravated between the Governments of Great Britain and the United States. This going to confiding emigrants with a lie in the mouth, deluding them from home on the promise of steady work and good pay, when the real intent is to make merchandize of them, is what all fair-minded men object to and repudiate. The pernicious maxim, "The end justifies the means," has not yet been consecrated as a permanent rule of action, and therefore they who seem to have adopted it must look to have their acts characterized by their appropriate names.

It appears by the concurrent statements of the men imported by Mr. Finney for

Mr. Kidder, at an expenditure of 1,100*l.*, that they were contracted to work on railroads and waterworks, at 2*l.* British per month (some say 10 dollars per month), and found, with free passage to the United States, one suit of clothes per year, and pay to commence immediately on arrival. It appears, on the other hand, by statements of Mr. Kidder, that he was unauthorized to contract with labourers for railroad work by any railroad Company; that he had no railroad work for the men; no waterworks work for them; and that his arrangement with Mr. McDonald, Contractor of the Charlestown Waterworks, was an afterthought, made after the men arrived, and made in consequence of the frustration of the great object for which the men were brought here. It is in evidence before the Committee that, on the passage to this country, when some of the men were talking with Mr. Finney about the contract they had entered into and the work they were to do, he replied to them that they might find themselves shouldering a musket on their arrival. One of the men is deficient of an eye. Finney did not know of the deficiency until the vessel was on its passage. When he discovered the fact he denounced the man as having cheated him in not making his deformity known—as though the loss of an eye would incapacitate a man for railroad work.

The first experience of the men on their arrival in Portland is significant of the real object for which they were imported. If Finney, as the agent of Kidder, really brought them over under contract to Kidder to work on railroads at a stipulated rate, each man of them having cost Kidder 70 dollars (his own statement), it is only reasonable to suppose that Finney would have used ordinary diligence, to say the least, to keep the men together under his supervision until he could deliver them over to his principal, and use more than ordinary diligence in preventing persons from enticing away the men upon whom his employer had already expended so much money. Instead of that, however, we find him inviting recruiting agents to circulate among his charge, to be free with their liquor, to use their influence to divert them from the professed object he engaged them for. We find him on terms of excellent understanding with the policemen of that city, and that, after a number of his company had been taken to the station-house—after enjoying whiskey hospitality which had been so freely tendered to all—he leaves word that the men may be released at once if they will enlist; if they will not, that they cannot be released until he says so. Eight or ten did enlist under these circumstances, yet we hear of no word of apology from Mr. Finney to Mr. Kidder for this carelessness of men committed to his charge, who had already cost Kidder 70 dollars each, or of complaint from Kidder to Finney for breach of contract and orders, and for general neglect, by which Kidder not only ran the risk of losing his expenses, but—what must be of far greater consequence, if his explanation that he wanted labourers is correct—the loss of his men. We would like to see the settlement of the accounts concerning the men who enlisted at Portland, that we might know how much Mr. Kidder loses or gains by that transaction.

But Mr. Kidder, in a card published in the "Daily Advertiser," copied into the "Courier," affirms that he caused the men to be brought over here as an "an experiment to see if by possibility a plan of importing labourers could be made self-sustaining." He adds, "The depth of poverty from which this hundred men have been taken may be inferred from the fact that before they were shipped they all signed an agreement to work for one year for 10 dollars a-month and their board and lodging—the cost of their passage to be deducted from their first earnings." There was a contract, then? Yet Mr. Kidder admitted to the Committee that even before the men had arrived he was in consultation with the recruiting agent of the 28th Regiment in reference to them. It is also admitted, and not denied by any one, that, in his first interview with the men, on the very night of their arrival in Charlestown, Mr. Kidder addressed them, said they had come upon him unawares, work was not ready for all of them, but if any would like to enlist they could do so at once, and suggested the 28th Regiment as a desirable regiment to enter. This does not look like an over anxiety to see if the "plan of importing labourers could be made self-sustaining," but "wicey warcey—quite the rewarse," as Captain Cuttle would say.

The insinuation of Mr. Kidder about the depth of poverty from which the men have been rescued by his philanthropic labours is ungracious and unkind, and, what is more, it is untrue. He may not be aware of the fact, but it is in evidence before the Committee that the men, as a body, were industrious mechanics and labourers of the city of Dublin, more than ordinarily intelligent, all of them able-bodied, with the exception of the one-eyed man, whom Finney swore at for cheating him, and all of them were in employment in their respective callings, earning from 15*s.* to 1*l.* 10*s.* a-week wages. But the most noticeable part of Mr. Kidder's card is the complaint that "the conduct of the men on this occasion will no doubt preclude the probability of any further attempts of the kind being made," and the admission that "I am informed, on the best authority, that 10,000 men could be engaged on the same terms as these." The complaint and the admission are both important as showing, on the one hand, what progress had been made in this emigration scheme in Ireland; and, on the other, how completely it has been frustrated by "the conduct of the men," and the disclosures that have been made "on this occasion."

We wait the Report of the Committee, the substance of which, and the conclusions which the meeting may arrive at, we shall publish. It was designed that the Report should be made this evening, but an unavoidable postponement has been made to Friday evening.

No. 7.

Earl Russell to Lord Lyons.

My Lord,   Foreign Office, April 5, 1864.

I HAVE received from Consul Murray a copy of his despatch to you of the 17th ultimo, respecting seven Irishmen forming a portion of the emigrants taken to America by Finney, who, on their arrival at Portland, were improperly induced to enter the United States' military service; and I have to instruct you to apply to Mr. Seward for the release of these men.

I am, &c.
(Signed)   RUSSELL.

No. 8.

Lord Lyons to Earl Russell.—(Received April 24.)

My Lord,   Washington, April 8, 1864.

WITH reference to my despatches to your Lordship of the 14th and 22nd ultimo, I have the honour to transmit to your Lordship copies of further papers relative to the enlistment at Portland and Boston of Irish immigrants who arrived at the former place on board the packet "Nova Scotian" on the 9th ultimo.

It appears that an investigation of the circumstances under which the enlistment took place at Portland is going on that place, and that Her Majesty's Consul has been invited to be present, and attends daily. I regret, however, to say that I find that my request that these men might not be sent forward to the army pending the investigation has not been attended to. One of them, Thomas Tulley, has called at this Legation, and has written the statement which forms the 12th inclosure in this despatch. It seems that he and his companions were forwarded to the army of the Potomac, that the others are now serving in the 20th Maine Regiment in that army, and that he himself would also be in actual service in that regiment had he not been sent back to the hospital here on account of illness.

I observe in the report of a speech of a Mr. Edward Ryan, which appears in the newspaper extract (Inclosure 7 in this despatch), a statement that Mr. Murray, Her Majesty's Consul at Portland, had refused to interfere in the case of a man named Martin Hogan. The name of Martin Hogan appears, however, among the names of the men in whose behalf Mr. Murray appealed to the local authorities, and in whose behalf I, acting on a report from Mr. Murray, appealed to the United States' Government. The insinuation made by the same speaker that Mr. Murray "makes money himself in the recruiting business" is of course simply absurd.

I have, &c.
(Signed)   LYONS.

Inclosure 1 in No. 8.

Consul Lousada to Lord Lyons.

My Lord,   Boston, March 21, 1864.

IN continuation of the case of Irishmen brought over to this country by Finney (subject of my despatch of the 18th instant) I now have the honour to inclose a leading article of to-day's "Courier," which logically confutes the sophistry of Mr. Kidder's "card," and will repay perusal, as really setting forth the true nature of the transaction. The final action of the Committee is postponed until Friday, and I shall be able by the subsequent mail to report the result.

I have not as yet succeeded in getting a list of the men, but expect to do so. Copies of this article as well as of the previous ones were sent by me to the Foreign Office.

After writing thus far, I received a letter of which I inclose a copy. This letter contained an inclosure (original transmitted herewith, with request that it may be returned at once after perusal in order that I may restore it to owner).

My reason for forwarding this document is, that it forcibly strikes me as being a ramification of what I consider the same plot against our labouring men; for to entice them over under pretence of remunerative work, and then to put them in the position of either being in want or of enlisting, is to all intents and purposes a nefarious conspiracy.

I have, &c.
(Signed)   F. LOUSADA.

Inclosure 2 in No. 8.

Extract from the " Courier."

[See Inclosure in No. 6.]·

Inclosure 3 in No. 6.

Mr. Ainsworth to Consul Lousada.

14, Pinfice Block, City of Lawrence, Massachusetts,
Sir,   March 19, 1864.
HAVING come to this country on July 22, 1863, on the steamer "Georgia," I beg to ask you for a passage back to my own country. My object in coming to this country was to open a field of labour for my suffering countrymen in Blackburn. I am sorry to give you to understand that I have not been able to carry my plan into effect for want of health. I inclose a letter in this that will show you my intended route to this country and Canada, but I hope you will have the kindness to send the inclosed letter back with a reply; the gentlemen of this country having sent for my family, thinking I would have better health, but I am sorry to inform you that the climate is against me, and I beg of you to grant a passage for my family as well, as all my means and money is done.

Your obedient servant,
(Signed)   H. W. AINSWORTH.

Inclosure 4 in No. 6.

Mr. Stuart to Mr. Buchanan.

Canadian Government Information Office, 19, Drury Buildings,
Water Street, Liverpool, July 7, 1863, at the
Dear Sir,   landing-stage, Tuesday morning.
THIS will introduce to you Mr. H. W. Ainsworth from Blackburn. Mr. Ainsworth proceeds to our country as a delegate from an important Emigration Committee, the only one of the populous manufacturing town of Blackburn. Mr. Ainsworth will present you with a letter from his Committee; he has awoke my special interest as a man earnestly interested in behalf of his suffering countrymen. I will leave him fully to open up to you the special object of his visit to Canada, and as he proceeds or intend to proceed from New York to Quebec, very much, if not for the express purpose of seeing Mr. Buchanan, whose name is regarded in this country as that of one who must be a friend to the people, I trust you will be able to put Mr. Ainsworth in the right road of introducing the subject personally to the kind consideration of our Government and people.

Mr. King, Editor of the " Blackburn Times," arranged with the Messrs. J. Bains and Co., to have·this, the second party from Blackburn to Canada this season, to go by the " Albion " screw-steamer to New York (passages 4l. 10s.); the first party left here by same route last Tuesday (some thirty in number), and this party of over thirty go ot-day. A good journey to them, and a welcome to Canada.
(Signed)   W. F. STEWART.

Inclosure 5 in No. 6.

Consul Lousada to Lord Lyons.

My Lord,   Boston, March 23, 1864.
IN continuation of my despatch of the 21st instant on the subject of those imported Irishmen, I have the honour to report that Finney came to my office to-day, and a more villainous specimen of humanity, as far as outward signs go, I have rarely seen; just the

tool fitted for the work. He had the audacity to affect to consult me as to whether he could not arrest these men for breach of their contract with him, and said he was going on to Washington to see the Secretary of War, to claim from him the men already enlisted to his (Finney's) detriment.

He professes ignorance as to the whereabouts of the bulk of the importation (the list of which as procured from Portland herewith inclosed); but he admits that several have enlisted, and that he got one off in the 4th Massachusetts Cavalry, which sailed to day for Hilton Head.

After leaving, he came back again, and with a look of inexpressibly low cunning asked me, in case he succeeded in reclaiming his men from the Secretary of War, what action I propose to take in the matter. I simply told him it would be time enough to consider that when the case arose.

I have, &c.
(Signed)　　　F. LOUSADA.

Inclosure 6 in No. 8.

Consul Lousada to Lord Lyons.

My Lord,　　　　　　　　　　　　　　　　　　*Boston, March 26, 1864.*
I HAVE the honour to inclose copies of the Report of the Committee of Investigation in the Irish emigration case. The meeting stands adjourned, but I doubt if any further action will be taken.

I have, &c.
(Signed)　　　F. LOUSADA.

Inclosure 7 in No. 8.

Report of the Committee of Investigation in the Irish Emigration Case.

THE KIDDER EMIGRANTS. REPORT OF THE COMMITTEE OF INVESTIGATION.—AN adjourned meeting of citizens, called to consider the treatment of certain Irish emigrants who lately arrived in Boston in the steamer "Nova Scotian," at Portland, was held in the Hall of the Democratic Club last evening. The Committee appointed to investigate the case came in with their Report, in which they say that they have examined publicly a great number of witnesses, and have also had communications with various persons in relation to the matter. The Committee direct their attention in the first place to the alleged ill-treatment and neglect suffered by the emigrants from those who had them in charge, and they have gathered the following facts:—that the emigrants are all healthy, able-bodied young men, and nearly all able to read and write; that during the time they were in Portland, and up to 9 o'clock of the evening of the 9th, it does not appear they received any attentions from the persons whose duty it was to provide for them, neither shelter nor food having been given to them; that Mr. Kidder caused them to be brought to a vacant store in Bunker Hill Street, Charlestown, on the night of their arrival from Portland, and there, after having provided them with crackers, cheese, tea, ale, and whiskey, left them to pass a winter's night on the bare floor, without even a blanket to cover them, and at an hour when, for half a dollar a-piece at the utmost, comfortable lodgings could be provided for each of them; that there were no proper efforts made by persons claiming control of the men to provide for them decently, to give them immediate employment, to keep them from indulging in intoxicating liquor, or to prevent them from falling into the hands of the "substitute brokers" and "runners" for recruiting offices, who gathered about the emigrants and entrapped a number of them into enlisting; that had it not been for the kindness of the good people of Charlestown, who provided them with every assistance that could be afforded, the emigrants would have suffered still worse than they did; and finally, that both Finney and Kidder, together with all concerned, must acknowledge that the emigrants were not treated by them as even the common usages of civilization demand that human beings should be treated.

In reference to the allegations that the object in bringing the emigrants to this country was to induce them to enter the military service of the United States as a part of the quota of Massachusetts, the Committee say, "For the purpose of leaving the public to judge of the truth of the matter alleged, we have embodied in our Report the statement of a number of witnesses, and thus leave every person to draw his own inference. The Committee add for themselves that, if the emigrants made any arrangement to enlist in the army when they arrived here, or had it been understood that they were to enlist, then those who induced them to come to this country cannot be charged with having practised any trick or deception upon them. But the men deny that it was intended they should enlist, and the principal parties engaged in bringing them to this country deny it also, and furthermore say that the whole aim in inducing the men to emigrate was a philanthropic project, something intended to better the condition of the men and to benefit the State.

Among the persons examined was one of the emigrants, Michael Kirby. He states that, while on the passage Finney said to him, in conversation, "Tell them (the other emigrants) that they had better be prepared to take the musket when they land." Before this the men had begun to have suspicions that they were intended for the United States' service, by what the firemen and stewards said. This witness testified at length respecting their experience after the arrival in Portland and down to the time when the men were lodged in Kidder's old building in Charlestown. It was then that Kidder himself came among them and made a speech on the occasion, saying among other things, "If you have a mind to enlist I would advise you to enlist in the 28th Regiment," but saying nothing about work he had for them to do. Simeon Gavin, another of the emigrants, testified that Kidder's first conversation with them was to enlist with him (Kidder) as he was entitled to enlist the men, having brought them out. Finney up to this time had never cautioned any of the men against enlisting. Gavin came over to Boston the next day, and he with companions, by some means found themselves in the Harbour Police Station, and he gives a curious history of the various and persistent efforts that were made to induce them to enlist.

Mr. Finney, himself, was then examined by the Committee at great length. He says, he has lived thirteen years in this country, and has passed most of the time between Haverhill, Manchester and Northfield. He has never been engaged either directly or indirectly in enlisting men for the army. He explains his introduction to Kidder in this wise : He met an Irishman from Portland, whose name he has forgotten, who had just come from Kidder's office, and was told by him that a number of Irishmen were to be imported to this country. Finney thought he would try for a chance. He don't know how he came to speak to the Portland man. He and another (both were Irishmen) were talking, when Finney came up, about bringing over emigrants and paying their passage, and about parties in town who were to do it. "I can't say whether the stranger mentioned Kidder's name first, or myself." In relation to his interview with Kidder, Finney distinctly states that his object in calling upon that gentleman was to get him to contribute something to bring emigrants over. He proposed to get them from Galway. He told Kidder he was about to start a project himself to get men over. Referred Mr. K. to John B. Chase, and Dr. Tibbetts, Manchester, N. H., and William Jeffers, Haverhill. Was simply asking for the means to get the men out, and considered the project his own individual undertaking. On the next day, Mr. Kidder said he knew a firm who would take hold and help in the undertaking, and then gave him a copy of an agreement for each man to sign to work for me (Finney) for one year, at 10 dollars a month and board and lodging :—the work to be done on the Charlestown Water Works, Pennsylvania Coal Mine, Hartford and Erie Railroad, &c. Mr. Kidder's name was not mentioned in the agreement. My compensation was to be 50 dollars a month. In a conversation Finney had with Governor Andrew, he told the Governor what Kidder and the others were doing. The Governor replied, he would have nothing to do with it. He had no money to invest.

In reference to his arrest in Ireland, Finney said his papers were all right, and the authorities could make nothing of them. The papers were simply four or five letters from contractors who said they wanted them. One of the men, Pat McDermott, him with a lame eye, stated to the Committee, in the presence of Finney, that Finney one day accosted him on ship-board, in the roughest manner, swearing,—"I have been rightly sucked in by you." The way that he had been sucked in was, that McDermott kept the peak of his cap over his blind eye so that Finney should not see it. Finney denied to the Committee that such a scene took place, or such language was used.

The statement of Kidder was given by the Committee above almost *verbatim*. He was examined nearly three hours. He stated that Finney had been recommended to him as a respectable Irishman. His sole object in engaging in the undertaking was to do a good deal of good at a small outlay. His instructions to Finney were to hire men for labour and nothing else, and say nothing about war, else he might get into difficulty with the Government. Finney was to be paid according to the success of the scheme—liberally if it was very successful. It had proved a total failure, and he would be paid nothing. He had asked some gentlemen who participated in the Board of Trade Emigration meeting a few months ago to associate with him, but they had refused. Finney had orders only for 100 men. Another gentleman, Mr. Ames, was concerned with him in the enterprise, and he has to bear half the loss. Governor Andrew knew of the matter, but could not act officially in regard to it. Orders were sent not to ship any of the men after the 23rd of February. When the men arrived, he told them if they wanted to enlist they could do so, but he wanted the 70 dollars each man had cost out of their bounty. In anticipation of their arrival had tried to get work for them, but arranged nothing definite.

The Report concludes by calling public attention to the part the Portland and Boston police had acted in endeavouring to get these men to enlist.

Martin Lynch called attention to some points that had been omitted by the Committee. Kidder acknowledged he had applied to a recruiting office in regard to these men before they arrived. Another point : The treatment some of the men have received from the Boston police. He charged it distinctly that a member of the harbour police arrested two men for drunkenness; that he, with others, tried every art and inducement to have them enlist ; that on their release the next morning this same policeman said, "You look cold, my boys," and took them to a bar room, treated them three or four times, and paid for the drinks. The policeman denied the fact, denied that he had left the Station-house when the men left; but Mr. Lynch traced him with the men to a bar-room, where the men drank. And he wanted the meeting to understand and know that there is such a thing in Boston as a policeman taking a man up for drunkenness at night, and taking him out the next morning and giving him drink three or four times.

Mr. Lynch had not the slightest doubt that Mr. Kidder brought the men over for the purpose of enlisting them. Why, else, did he make no arrangements to receive them? Why, else, did he apply to a recruiting officer concerning them before they arrived? Mr. Lynch also said that he had been informed by a lawyer of Boston that Kidder had stated before the men arrived that he was engaged in a recruiting scheme which, if successful, would soon fill up the quota of Boston. Mr. Lynch did not hesitate to say that the whole thing was a rascally operation, turn it which way you will.

Eneas Smyth, Esq., noticed the contradictions between the statements of Mr. Kidder and Mr. Finney, and examined the statements of both at some length. He made no question that, instead of this being a philanthropic scheme, as claimed Mr. Kidder, it was a scheme to make money, either in the difference of wages between 10 dollars a month and board, the sum they were to receive from Kidder, and the wages their labour would actually bring, or by enlisting them.

Mr. Edward Ryan would have the Report amended by censuring severely those men in Boston and Portland who were so actively officious in urging the emigrants to enlist. As to Messrs. Kidder and Finney, whatever their intentions were, they had worked their cards too shrewdly to authorize us to say, definitely, they had been engaged in a scheme of enlistment. At any rate it was perfectly plain that Irishmen here had been foremost in endeavouring to get recruiting bounties for them. He stated that he had just returned from Portland and was convinced from what he had heard, that the men who were enlisted in Portland were drugged and forced into the army by the authorities of that city. The case of Martin Hogan, one of these emigrants, was one of peculiar outrage and hardship. He was a stucco-worker by trade and had engaged to work for a plasterer at 3 dollars a day. One day, while at his employment, a man came and told him some of his chums were on the Railroad Wharf and wanted to see him. He went, saw none of his chums, but found a man who claimed to know him, who invited him into a bar-room, where he drank one glass, and the next thing he knew was he found himself, next morning, in Camp Berry. He has refused to receive the bounty, refused to put on the military clothing, and even refused to eat the camp rations, having pledged his watch to supply himself with food, yet that man cannot be released from the camp. · The British Consul at Portland has refused to interfere, for the reason, Mr. Ryan thought, that he makes money himself in the substitute business. Hogan has a wife in Dublin. He fears that he will be sent away in a day or two in a transport. The attention of Lord Lyons has been called to this case. Mr. Ryan concluded by hoping there would be embodied in the Report of the Committee a severe censure upon the authorities of Portland for their connivance in kidnapping these men.

Other remarks were made, when the suggestion of Mr. Ryan was adopted, and the meeting adjourned.

Inclosure 8 in No. 8.

Mr. Seward to Lord Lyons.

My Lord,   *Department of State, Washington, March* 28, 1864.
    I HAVE the honour to acknowledge the receipt of your communication of the 19th
instant, respecting the cases of Thomas Tulley, Michael Byrne, James Higgins, Edward
Cassidy, Thomas Burke, Michael Moran, and Martin Hogan, alleged to be British subjects,
and to have been improperly enlisted into the United States' army.
    I have the honour to inform your Lordship that I have invited the early attention of
the Secretary of War to these cases, and have requested him to cause an investigation
thereof, and the adoption of such proceeding as the result may seem to require.
    If the report of a similar transaction at Philadephia,* mentioned by your Lordship,
should prove to be well-founded, I shall cheerfully adopt the same course in regard to it,
when I shall have received the names of the men and such details as you may be able to
communicate to me.
                              I have, &c.
                    (Signed)   WILLIAM H. SEWARD.

Inclosure 9 in No. 8.

Consul Murray to Lord Lyons.

My Lord,   *Portland, March* 28, 1864.
    IN acknowledging the receipt of your Lordship's despatch dated respectively the
18th and 19th instant, I have the honour to report that the Provost-Marshal at Portland,
Captain Doughty, received on the 17th instant an order from the Acting Assistant
Provost-Marshal-General, Major Gardiner, to make an investigation of the circumstances
under which the seven Irishmen who were landed from the steam-ship " Nova Scotian "
on the 9th instant were enlisted into the United States' military service.
    The examination of the witnesses, under this order, commenced on the 25th instant,
and is continued daily at the office of the Provost-Marshal.
    Having received an invitation from Captain Doughty to be present at these examina-
tions, I have availed myself of the permission, and have been in daily attendance. I will
report again to your Lordsoip on their conclusion.
                              I have, &c.
                    (Signed)   HENRY JOHN MURRAY.

Inclosure 10 in No. 8.

Lord Lyons to Mr. Seward.

Sir,   *Washington, April* 7, 1864.
    IN a note which I had the honour to address to you on the 19th of last month, I
called your attention to the circumstances under which seven British subjects had (as I
was informed) been entrapped into the United States' army immediately after they
landed at Portland, and at the same time I expressed my hope that if the men were not
discharged at once measures would be immediately taken to prevent their being
forwarded to the army or placed in actual service pending an investigation of the matter.
You were so good as to inform me in reply, in a note dated the 28th of last month, that
you had invited the early attention of the Secretary of War to the case of those men.
I am very anxious to learn as soon as possible what has been done with the men, and I
am also desirous of being made acquainted with any proceedings which may have been
adopted with a view to investigate the circumstances connected with their enlistment.
    In the note to which I have referred I also informed you that it had been reported
to me that a large number of Irishmen, brought over by the same packet, and in charge
of the same person, a man named Finney, had been practised on in a not unsimilar
manner in the neighbourhood of Boston.
    I have herewith the honour to inclose a list of the names of the passengers by the
packet in question, the " Nova Scotian." I have not yet received special information

* Qy. Boston.

respecting any of these men individually excepting the seven enlisted at Portland. But it is reported to me by Her Majesty's Consul at Boston that several of them have been enlisted. The treatment to which a great number of them were subjected in the neighbourhood of Boston has become matter of public notoriety; and I cannot doubt that the proper authorities will consider that there is, to .say the least, sufficient *primâ facie* evidence that these men have been unfairly dealt with, to render it proper that steps should be taken to trace those of them who have enlisted, and at the same time to investigate thoroughly the circumstances under which their enlistment took place.

I must, moreover, express my hope that the United States' Government will take into consideration the suggestion which I ventured to make in my note, that measures should be adopted to protect foreigners arriving in the United States from the practice of unscrupulous recruiting agents.

I have, &c.
(Signed) LYONS.

Inclosure 11 in No. 8.

Lord Lyons to Consul Lousada.

Sir,   *Washington, April 7, 1864.*
WITH reference to your despatches of the 11th, 12th, 17th, 21st, 23rd, and 26th ultimo, and to my despatch of the 13th ultimo, I have to state to you that I have represented to the Secretary of State of the United States that there is sufficient *primâ facie* evidence that a considerable number of the Irish passengers by the "Nova Scotia" were unfairly dealt with, to render it proper that measures should be taken by the proper authorities to trace those who have enlisted in the United States' army, and to investigate thoroughly the circumstances under which their enlistment took place.

You will bear in mind my instruction of the 13th ultimo, and not relax your own endeavours to trace these men, and to obtain in the several cases such evidence of the practices by which they were made to enlist as may serve to support applications from me to the United States' Government for their discharge.

I have suggested to the Secretary of State of the United States that effectual measures should be taken to protect British subjects arriving in the United States from the practices of unscrupulous recruiting agents.

I am, &c.
(Signed) LYONS.

Inclosure 12 in No. 8.

Petition of Thomas Tulley.

No. 5 Ward, Finley Hospital, Washington, Delaware County,
May it please your Lordship,   *April 4, 1864.*
THE humble petition of Thomas Tulley, one of Her Britannic Majesty's subjects, but now enrolled in D Company 20th Maine Regiment, United States' army, humbly solicits your Lordship's kind consideration and perusal of the following petition. Your Lordship's Petitioner came from Liverpool in the steam-ship "Nova Scotian," and landed in Portland on the 9th of last month, for the purpose of fulfilling a lucrative employment in the establishment of Messrs. Page, Richardson and Co., of Boston, but the day he landed he missed the cars, and, after being about six hours in America, Petitioner was confined in the city prison.

That Petitioner was visited in his cell the next morning by a recruiting Agent and asked to enlist, and thereby gain his liberty; this Petitioner refused, and remonstrated with the Agent as to such conduct in a civilized country.

That Petitioner was suffering with thirst and hunger, and he applied to the prison officials for sustenance, which was refused. Petitioner then demanded to be brought before a Magistrate, but he was informed that he would be brought before no such person. Petitioner then asked when he would get his liberty, but his question was met with a dubious answer, but that if Petitioner enlisted he would be released and get plenty of food and drink.

That Petitioner, under the circumstances, asked for his liberty in order that he might consider the matter fully, hoping to get to the British Consul. The Deputy Governor unlocked the cell-door, but Petitioner was met at the main entrance to the prison and presented with enlisting papers, which he refused to sign, when your Petitioner was again locked up. Subsequently Petitioner was again assailed by Army Agents, and one of them took your Petitioner to a recruiting office, watched by the police, who had orders to bring your Petitioner back to prison unless he signed the enlisting papers, which Petitioner, under such circumstances, was compelled to sign, after which Petitioner received food and drink, but not his liberty. Petitioner was then locked in a room, where he received clothing, and was brought by an escort to the Treasury Office, where they gave Petitioner 200 dollars State bounty, the principal portion of which sum was extorted from Petitioner for paltry articles of clothing, &c.

That Petitioner on the evening of his enlistment and the day after his arrival in America was sent to Camp Berry, outside Portland, where he was again almost a prisoner, and Petitioner seeing his position managed through a friend to send a letter to Mr. Murray the British Consul, who came and investigated the matter before the Colonel in command at that place, and he signified his strong disapprobation of the manner I and five more of my countrymen were treated, as Petitioner begs to remind your Lordship that there are five more men who were treated in the same manner as Petitioner, and are now serving in the same company and regiment as your Petitioner. Mr. Murray informed Petitioner that he would apply to the Provost-General for Petitioner's and his companions' release, and that if he did not succeed he would lay the case before your Lordship; but whether he has done so or not, your Petitioner is ignorant of. Mr. Murray also advised your Petitioner to take no more money, and when the Government bounty 173 dollars was offered, your Petitioner refused taking it, although the other five men took it, so that your Lordship's Petitioner has taken no money except the State bounty as aforesaid, which he was almost forced to take.

That on Petitioner's march through the country he posted a letter for your Lordship in Philadelphia, but Petitioner fears it did not reach your Lordship.

That on Petitioner's arrival at his regiment which forms part of the army of the Potomac, he was sent back to this hospital on account of some slight sickness, and under such a fortunate event Petitioner is able to lay his case before your Lordship before he is again sent back, and Petitioner fully hopes that your Lordship will get your Petitioner his liberty, on account of the unlawful manner he has been treated in America.

That your Petitioner was about representing the matter to the Secretary of State in London, and also to the two members who represent his native city in Parliament, but having thought of your Lordship as Representative of England in America, Petitioner once more craves your Lordship's interference with the War Department, and thereby obtain your Petitioner's release.

That your Petitioner has served his own country for many years during the Indian mutiny, and is at present receiving sevenpence per day pension, having been discharged on account of bad sight, but a good chance having offered I came to America to better my position, and scarcely was Petitioner landed in free America than he was treated as aforesaid, but which I am certain your Lordship will not tolerate.

That your Petitioner is prepared to make an affidavit before any person as to the foregoing statement.

Your Petitioner therefore humbly prays that your Lordship will do whatever is necessary for your Petitioner.

And in duty bound your Lordship's Petitioner will ever pray.

(Signed)   THOMAS TULLEY,
D Company 20th Maine Regiment.

P.S.—Your Lordship's Petitioner is likely to be shortly sent back to his regiment. Will your Lordship, therefore, attend to your Petitioner's case shortly, and for which may you have every blessing.

T. T.

Inclosure 13 in No. 8.

Lord Lyons to Mr. Seward.

Sir,   *Washington, April 8, 1864.*
WITH reference to the note which I had the honour to address to you yesterday, I regret to say that I have learned that Thomas Tulley and five of the men enlisted

at Portland, whose cases I represented to you on the 19th of last month, were sent to the army of the Potomac, and enrolled in Company D, of the 20th Maine Regiment. Five of them are, as I understand, actually serving in that regiment in the field or in camp. Tulley has, I am informed, been transferred temporarily to the Finley Hospital in this city. I deem it right, therefore, again to call your attention to the request I made on the 19th ultimo, that these men might not be forwarded to the army, nor placed in actual service, pending an investigation of the circumstances of their enlistment.

I have, &c.
(Signed)   LYONS.

No. 9.

Lord Lyons to Earl Russell.—(Received May 1.)

My Lord,   *Washington, April* 19, 1864.
    WITH reference to my despatch of the 8th instant, and to the previous correspondence relative to the enlistment at Portland and Boston of the Irish passengers by the steamer "Nova Scotian," I have the honour to transmit to your Lordship herewith a copy of a note from Mr. Seward, acknowledging the receipt of my communications of the 7th and 8th instant on the subject.
    I have also the honour to transmit to your Lordship copies of a despatch from Mr. Consul Murray, and of its inclosures. The inclosures consist of a Report of the Provost Marshal and Board of Enrolment at Portland, and of depositions on which it is in part founded.
    I shall endeavour to obtain further information from the enlisted men themselves, as the Report of the Board does not appear to me to be conclusive as to their having been fairly dealt with.

I have, &c.
(Signed)   LYONS.

Inclosure 1 in No. 9.

Mr. F. Seward to Lord Lyons.

My Lord,   *Department of State, Washington, April* 12, 1864.
    I HAVE the honour to acknowledge the receipt of your communication of the 7th and 8th instant, referring to that of the 19th of last month, relative to the case of Thomas Tulley, Michael Byrne, and five other Irishmen, British subjects, said to have improperly enlisted into the United States' military service, and the former relating also to the alleged treatment of the passengers of the "Nova Scotian," and to the subject of the practices of recruiting agents in regard to foreigners arriving in this country. I have the honour to inform your Lordship, in reply, that I have inclosed a copy of those communications to the Secretary of War, whose particular attention has been drawn to the request contained therein.

I have, &c.
(Signed)   F. W. SEWARD, *Acting Secretary.*

Inclosure 2 in No. 9.

Consul Murray to Lord Lyons.

My Lord,   *Portland, April* 7, 1864.
    I HAVE the honour to transmit herewith a duplicate Report, together with a set of duplicate sworn evidence, made by the Provost Marshal and Board of Enrolment at Portland, to Major Gardiner, the Acting Assistant Provost Marshal General at Augusta, in pursuance of instructions under date of the 17th ultimo, to investigate into the circumstances under which seven Irishmen had been enlisted into the military service of the United States; the official attention of Major Gardiner having been requested by a communication from myself dated the 14th ultimo, inclosing a copy of a petition addressed to me from these men, who alleged that they had been improperly and against their will, enlisted into the service.

I was present during the whole investigation, which lasted for several days, and I have much pleasure in testifying to the good faith and earnest endeavours of the Provost Marshal and his coadjutors in obtaining the most searching evidence.

The conclusion that the Board have come to is, that they "cannot learn that any one connected with recruiting furnished any liquor to these men. That food and drink were furnished to them while in confinement, such as is furnished to other prisoners in like circumstances. That they were enlisted of their own free will while perfectly sober. That after their enlistment they never refused to enter the service when brought before the Provost Marshal, and therefore were never returned to confinement for refusing. That two watches were sold to them by men in United States' uniforms, as will appear by the statements of Lieutenant Strout and Sergeant Atkinson, and nothing else."

As this conclusion is based upon the personal knowledge of the Board, and upon sworn testimony, while the written allegations of the absent Irishmen are somewhat confused, and do not contain the whole truth, it will be difficult to rebut it. Yet a perusal of the evidence will prove that some portion of their complaint was not without reason.

The Board state no one connected with recruiting furnished any liquor to the men. This may be true, or at least there may be no evidence to prove the fact as regards those identical men, but there can be no doubt that there was a systematic attempt made to get these emigrants drunk for the purpose of enlistment. Policeman Berrick's evidence on this subject is most important. He states, "While in Mr. Bradley's (liquor store) there were two or three well-dressed men, I do not know their names, but have seen them in this city, who appeared to be liberal with their money. These men were not drinking themselves, but the emigrants were. I saw a man who said he was from Augusta, who appeared to be talking with the men out on the railroad track. This man said to me he was a recruiting officer, and wanted some of my help to get some of the men. I told him the police had nothing to do with business of that kind. He insinuated to me that if the men wanted liquor to aid them in getting it. I told him no, that I did not drink myself and would not assist in procuring any for the men."

Mr. Bradley, the keeper of the public-house testifies, that "a man came into my shop and bought a demijohn of whiskey; he carried it towards the wharf where the steamship lay. This man was a Canadian. He told me so. I have seen him before, don't know his name."

The evidence of these two persons is conclusive that the emigrants were treated to liquor; that the expected result took place—they got drunk, and some of them were conveyed to the Station-house; and that had they not been made drunk, they would have gone off to Boston with their companions.

. The charge of intimidation is founded, I presume, upon the evidence of police officer Cole, who states that when they asked him what would be their punishment for getting drunk and for riotous behaviour, replied that they would be fined thirty shillings sterling, or be liable to imprisonment for thirty days. This may be the law, but I much doubt whether it is carried out in practice.

The evidence given by the police officers and the recruiting officers proves that there was a very good understanding between these functionaries, and that the latter were even called and admitted to the cells with the object of inducing the men to enlist.

The charge of having watches and jewellery palmed off upon them by persons in the uniform of the United States is met by the statement of Lieutenant Strout and Serjeant Atkinson, who, while they admit having sold them two watches at their earnest request, declare that also, at their desire, they accompanied the men to the watchmakers and other shops to make purchases, as it is not permitted to new recruits to go about by themselves.

With regard to Thomas Tulley, if due credit be given to the evidence of policeman Berrick, it would appear that he came over with the object of enlisting, not caring on which side he fought, but only for the party who gave him most money. I must however remark, on his behalf, that I understand on his leaving Camp Berry, he and one other of his companions refused to accept a portion of the bounty money due to them.

Major McClellan has not thought proper to acknowledge the receipt of my communication of the 14th ultimo, and I have been given to understand that he does not intend to do so, as he objects to the tone of it.

I have, &c.
(Signed) · HENRY JOHN MURRAY.

E

Inclosure 3 in No. 9.

Report.

Provost Marshal's Office, Portland, April 2, 1864.

WE have the honour to make the following report, as to the circumstances under which Thomas Tulley, Michael Byrne, James Higgins, Michael Moran, Edward Cassidy, Thomas Burke, and Martin Hogan, were enlisted at this office. This report was called for by your communication of March 17, 1864. A copy of a communication to Honourable Jacob Mc Cellan, Mayor of this city, was furnished us, which we forward with this Report. This communication was written by Her Majesty's Consul at this port, Henry John Murray, Esq. We assumed that this communication was in the nature of a complaint, and our object has been to arrive at the truth or falsity of these charges, by the last testimony that could be procured. Her Majesty's Consul was invited to be present and take a part in the investigation, and we are pleased to say he has been present during the entire investigation and taken a part in the same, and while he has been faithful to the interests of the Government that he represents, the entire intercourse between him and this Board has been of the most pleasant character. While we had no express order to take the testimony of any individual in the case, we supposed that a grave question of international policy was at stake, and that our own report would be of more value, if we should forward the sworn testimony that we have taken in the case upon which our Report is partially based. Of course a certain portion of our Report is made up from our own knowledge, and no testimony other than that of this Board could be procured. We commenced the investigation on the morning of the 25th day of March, and continued from day to day, as the other business of the office would permit, until the final completion.

The steam-ship "Nova Scotian" arrived at this port on the morning of the 9th of March, bringing a large number of Irish steerage passengers. As to the contract that they had signed to go to Boston we have no authentic proof, but suppose that to be the case. The first knowledge that we had of these men is that they landed, and about half-past 10 o'clock went to the house of James Bradly, jun., and called for food; some of the men were intoxicated when they arrived there; those who had food had money with which to pay their bills, and did pay in English coin. Prior to this, as appears from the statement of James Bradly, jun., a man, who said he was from Canada, bought a demijohn of whiskey, and carried it down towards the wharf where these emigrants landed. We do not know whether any of this liquor was served out to the men or not. Thus far we have not been able to learn who furnished or paid for the liquor that they drank; quite a number of these passengers became drunk, noisy, and troublesome. The police tried to keep them quiet until they could be forwarded to Boston, but they did not succeed, and several were carried to the watch-house. The evidence of the several policemen is referred to show these facts. Thomas Tulley, Michael Byrne, James Higgins, and Michael Moran, and other men who were not mustered into the United States' service, were among the men arrested by the police. As to their treatment while in the watch-house see the testimony of the police. We refer to the testimony of John Collins, recruiting officer, as to the condition of the three first named at the time of enlistment.

We believe that these men were perfectly sober when enlisted by Mr. Collins, and that they enlisted into the contract to serve in the military service of the country voluntarily. Mr. Collins enlisted Tulley, Higgins, and Byrne, and one other who was rejected by the Board. At first Byrne was examined and rejected for some difficulty with his foot. He was very anxious to be accepted; stated that he had been in the British East India Service, and had marched and could march with perfect ease; and in proof of his having been a soldier took a musket and went through with the manual of arms with great precision. After mature deliberation and examination of the 34th section of circular, No. 1 series of 1864, the Board decided to accept him. Patrick Brophe, the other one who was enlisted by Mr. Collins, was rejected for varicose veins. He was very anxious to be accepted, and was very much disappointed when the Board decided to reject him. We do know that Thomas Tulley, James Higgins, and Michael Byrne were mustered into the service when perfectly sober and according to their own express desire. We know nothing about the enlistment of Burke, Cassidy, Moran, and Hogan; only from testimony of John M. Todd, a recruiting officer, whose statement accompanies this report, and of police officer Cole, whose statement corroborates Mr. Todd's in some particulars. We refer to the statement of Mr. Todd, and believe in its correctness. Burke and Cassidy were presented for examination the afternoon of the 9th, but the surgeon refused to examine them because they were intoxicated, and they were taken away; brought in the next day with Moran, and the three were examined and mustered. Hogan was examined and mustered the 11th day. At no time have any of these seven men ever refused or expressed the slightest objections to be examined or mustered, but, on the contrary, earnestly desired it. Hogan never was in confinement at all; therefore the whole complaint as to Hogan falls to the ground. Therefore, in conclusion, we say that we cannot learn that any one connected with recruiting furnished any liquor to those men; that food and drink was furnished to them while in confinement such as is furnished to other prisoners in like circumstances; that they were enlisted of their own free will while perfectly sober; that after their enlistment they never refused to enter the service when brought before the Provost-Marshal, and therefore were never returned to confinement for refusing; that two watches were sold to them by men in United States' uniform, as will appear by the statements of Lieutenant Strout and Sergeant Atkinson, and nothing else.

  Hoping that this Report is satisfactory we subscribe ourselves, &c.

   (Signed) CHARLES H. DOUGHTY, *Captain and Provost Marshal.*
        EDWARD S. MORRIS, *Commissioner.*
        CHAS. W. THOMAS, M.D., *Surgeon.*

Inclosure 4 in No. 9.

Statement of J. W. Collins.

MY name is John W. Collins. I am a recruiting officer for the city of Portland. On the morning of the 10th day of March I received information from Police Officer William Foster that if I would go up to the watch-house it was his impression that there was a man there in cell No. 5 who was desirous to enlist. I went to the cell No. 5 about 9 A.M., and asked the man if he wished to enlist. He told me he did, but would not in prison. This was Thomas Tulley. He represented himself from the county of Galway, Ireland. I said to him he would not be asked to enlist in prison: you are strangers and Irishmen, and far be it from me to take any advantage of you. Tulley then said he would come out, and did come out of his cell, walked about to the other cells for about half an hour, talking with his companions. He went back into the cell and said he would not enlist. He asked me what would be done with him. I told him I could not tell him. I then went to the Mayor's office, found there the City Marshal, J. S. Heald, and the Mayor of Portland. I said to Mr. Heald the men imprisoned were under the impression they were prisoners, and would not enlist. I thought if they were set a liberty I could enlist some of them. Mr. Heald said, I have no objection for you to take the men and do the best you can with them. The Mayor said he would not have the impression go abroad that we coerced men to enlist in the city of Portland under any consideration. The Mayor and Mr. Heald (the Marshal) told Police-officer Cole to go down and liberate the men. He did so. The men were going out the back door. I told them no, that was the watch-house door; come upstairs, out through the City Building, at the front door. They did so. The men were perfectly sober. They told me they were dry and hungry. When they came out of the front door I said to them, There, men, you are at liberty to go where you please, but if you are desirous of enlisting give me the preference; I will do as well by you as any other recruiting agent will; I will guarantee that you have every cent that belongs to you. I showed them where the recruiting-office was that I kept. Thomas Tulley, James Higgins, and Michael Byrne followed me down and went in. They wanted some liquor. I said to them that I had taken solemn oath that I would not give any man as much liquor as would write his name to any man to induce him to enlist. I repeated this to them several times. After they found that I would not furnish them with liquor they consulted among themselves for about half an hour, and asked me to fill their papers. Tulley signed them first, then Byrne, then Higgins. They enlisted about half-past 11 o'clock in the forenoon. From the time they were discharged till the time they were enlisted they were perfectly free to come or go where they chose. If they had wished to see the British Consul they had perfect freedom to do so. If they had asked me to accompany them to the British Consul I should have done so. I took the three men up to the Provost Marshal's office. Tulley and Higgins were accepted. Byrne was at first rejected for a bunch on his foot, but he was very anxious to go; said he had been in the British service, and his foot did not trouble him.

The Board of Enrolment consulted together, and with Captain Lane of the 20th Regiment, and finally accepted him, and he was mustered in with Tulley and Higgins.

(Signed)   JOHN W. COLLINS.

State of Maine, Cumberland, ss., April 1, 1864.

Personally appeared John W. Collins, above-named, and made oath to the truth of the statement by him signed before me.

Signed before me,

(Signed)   EDWD. S. MORRIS, *Justice of the Peace.*

Inclosure 5 in No. 9.

Statement of John M. Todd.

MY name is John M. Todd; I reside in the city of Portland; am a recruiting officer. On the 9th day of March, while I was at dinner, about 12 o'clock, a serjeant and one other man came to my house and informed me they could bring me some men. When I went to my hair-dressing rooms, on Middle-street, I found them with Edward Cassidy, Thomas Burke, and Michael Moran. I enlisted, about 10 o'clock P.M., Burke and Cassidy. They were not intoxicated at the time. Moran refused to enlist at that time. I gave him my business-card that he might know where to go if he wanted to enlist afterwards. After Burke and Cassidy enlisted they went out with Sergeant Stewart and Robert Curran, and I did not see them again till half-past 3 o'clock, when Cassidy and Burke came back and wanted to go up to the Provost Marshal's Office and be examined. Cassidy was quite drunk. Burke was somewhat intoxicated when they came back. I went there with them.

The surgeon made a partial examination of Burke; Cassidy was so drunk that he would not examine him. Cassidy was so noisy that one of the police said he should arrest them if they went out into the street. They went below in the same building to the Police Office, and were locked up in the cells. Burke was not so drunk as Cassidy, but said he would not be separated from him; but if he was put in the lock-up he would go too. The next morning Robert Curran came to my shop and said the police wanted to see me at the office to take those men out. I went up to the cells; a man spoke to me and said, there is the man I agreed to go with, I have got his card. And he took the card I gave him out of his pocket. This was Moran, who was in my shop the day before. I took out the three men. I took Cassidy and Burke to the Provost Marshal's Office; they were examined and mustered. Moran went down to the shop; he enlisted there, came back to the Provost Marshal's Office, was examined and mustered. Moran was enlisted as soon as he got down to my office from the cell.

The afternoon of the 10th Martin Hogan was brought to me by Sergeant Stewart for enlistment. He was perfectly sober when he enlisted. I took him to the Provost Marshal's Office; but the Provost Marshal would not muster that afternoon, as he mustered men in the forenoon. Sergeant Stewart took him to the camp and kept him over night. Brought him to the Marshal's Office in the morning of the 11th, when he was mustered into service.

(Signed)   JOHN M. TODD.

State of Maine, Cumberland, ss., April 1, 1864.

Personally appeared John M. Todd and made oath to the truth of the above statement.

Before me,

(Signed)   EDWARD S. MORRIS, *Justice of the Peace.*

Inclosure 6 in No. 9.

Statement of H. G. Cole.

MY name is Harrison G. Cole. I am one of the police officers of the city of Portland; I have charge of the Station-house. I had charge of the station house on the 9th and 10th days of March, 1864, during the day. Deputy Marshal Wentworth had charge of the Station-house during the night of the days above-mentioned. My duties cease at 6 o'clock P.M., and commenced in the morning at half past 7 or 8 o'clock. On the afternoon of the 9th of March about half past 5 o'clock Edward Cassidy and Thomas Burke were brought to the Police Office by John M. Todd, a recruiting officer. One of them, I think Burke, was very drunk, the other was somewhat intoxicated—considerably so. Mr. Todd came to me before he brought the men, and said they were so drunk they would not examine them that afternoon, and asked me if I would lock them up and keep them till they were sober till the next morning. I understood him to mean that they would not be examined in the Provost Marshal's Office while they were drunk. I hesitated. I asked him where the men were. I told him if he would bring the men to me I would see whether I would lock them up or not. If they were drunk I would lock them up. He brought in Cassidy and Burke. I saw that they were both too drunk to be in the street. I told him I would lock them up and did. I saw no more of these men that night. Todd had no access to them that night, and no one else outside of the Police Office. Between half-past 8 and 9 the next morning Todd called for these men. He said he had enlisted these men on the day before and wanted them. He said they got drunk after he enlisted them. He claimed that he had enlisted them. He claimed that he had enlisted Mr. Moran, who was in the lock-up arrested by the police, and insisted upon taking him out. He produced before me a sergeant who he said brought the men to him to enlist. I discharged Moran and Cassidy and Burke, and he took them away. I think he shewed me enlisting papers, am not sure. They did not ask for food or water to my knowledge the evening they were locked up. The next morning between 8 and 9 o'clock I gave all the prisoners in the lock-up water myself several times, and crackers to all who wished. I do not recollect particularly about Moran, Cassidy, and Burke, whether they had food or not. They were discharged earlier than the other prisoners. These men would have been discharged by me by 10 o'clock in the morning if Todd had not called for them in company with the sergeant. They were taken charge of by me simply for the peace and order of the city, and for the safety of the men themselves. Thomas Tulley, Michael Byrne, and James Higgins, were brought to the office by the police on the afternoon of the 9th of March, between the hours of 12 and 3 o'clock. I was not in the office when they were brought in, but I saw them after they were locked up. They were very drunk and noisy. One of them was almost a maniac; he broke up the bucket in his cell and was very noisy. All of them were crazy drunk. No one outside of the office had access to them that afternoon, to my knowledge. I do not now remember that I gave them any food that afternoon. I gave them water several times. They did not ask for food. I think they asked for water. The next morning I went around, and gave them water and gave them crackers. Some of them refused to take the food offered—said they wanted breakfast. I replied to them that was the fare that the prisoners had. Before their discharge some of them expressed a wish to go on to Boston; some of them asked me what would be done with them as a punishment. I told them if they were brought before the Court they would be fined in sterling money about 1l. 10s. They replied to me they had no money. I told them if their agent would not pay their fine, they would be liable to imprisonment for thirty days; such is the law in such cases. A little after 9 o'clock, in conversation with Deputy Marshal Wentworth, I learned those men were not to be put before the Court. Something was said in the office, not in presence of the men, that some of them wished to enlist. Mr. Collins, a recruiting officer, came in, and asked me if there was not some men there who wanted to enlist. I replied I did not know whether there was or not. He asked me if he should go in to speak with the men. I told him I had no objection. He went in and talked with the men. I asked him what success he had. He said one wanted to enlist. I asked which one it was; he pointed out the man; I do not know which one it was; I am not positive, but think it was Higgins. I went to the man, and asked him if he wanted to enlist. He said he might as well enlist here as go to Boston and enlist. I gave him all the facts in relation to the bounty he would get. He said he wanted to get out of the place he was in; did not want to enlist there at any rate. I told him he could not enlist there at any rate. Then there was something said about what would be done with them if they did not enlist. I told them they probably would be holden there till their agent came for them at half-past 12 train. I had some conversation with the Deputy Marshal about turning them out. This man seemed to be anxious to enlist, and I discharged him after conversation with Deputy Wentworth. He went to the other men, and tried to persuade them to enlist. Finally some of them concluded to enlist. I told them they would not be forced to enlist if they were discharged. The men were all uneasy and wanted to get out. After further conversation with the Deputy, I discharged these men out of the cells, every one of them. I unlocked the cells of the whole of them; told each one of them that they were at liberty to do as they chose, only not to get drunk again and be brought back to the office. Then I showed them the way out; this between 10 and 11 o'clock A.M. Not one of these men have since been brought back to the police office except Michael Moran, who was arrested on suspicion as a deserter on March 11, at a house of ill fame in this city. Mr. Huse, a special agent from the Provost-Marshal's office, took him out of the lock-up March 12.

(Signed)   HARRISON G. COLE.

State of Maine, Cumberland, ss., April 1, 1864.

Personally appeared Harrison G. Cole above-named, and made oath to the truth of the statement by him signed.
> Before me,
> (Signed)   EDWARD S. MORRIS, *Justice of the Peace.*

Inclosure 7 in No. 9.

Statement of J. H. Bewick.

MY name is James H. Bewick. I am one of the police officers of Portland. I was the first officer present at the Grand Trunk depôt on the 9th of March, at the time of the riot of the steerage passengers of the "Nova Scotian." I was sent for by the agent who brought over the men ; was on the ground as early as 11 o'clock A.M. Mr. Floyd, who came after me, said that the agent wanted to keep the men from getting liquor. The most of the men were in Peter Bradley's liquor-shop. I went in Bradley's shop to look after the agent. I should think there were from twenty-five to forty in the shop; some were drinking—some were eating crackers and cheese. I did not find the agent. I stopped a few minutes—came out of the shop. The crowd appeared to gather around the shop of Bradley. I went from thence to the passenger depôt of the Grand Trunk Railway. I found the men there talking; one of them asked me if something could not be done to shut up the rum-shops (meaning P. H. Bradley's and others); that they were raising hell with the men. This man appeared to be an Englishman; from his conversation I supposed him to be one of the passengers who came in the same vessel.

Mr. Floyd pointed out the agent to me, who wanted me to assist him in keeping his men together till the train was ready for Boston. While we were talking, two or three men came up to him and wanted him to give them some liquor; he said, "No, not now; but after we get things righted we will see about it." While talking with him, some one called out for a fight. I made my way into the crowd and separated those men who were fighting. I went home to dinner for a few minutes; got back about half-past 12, and found a large number collected; then several other policemen were present. There was a great uproar. We tried to restrain them—put some of them into the freight depôt to keep them.

The great object of Deputy Marshal Wentworth and the police force was to keep them quiet, and get them off to Boston as quietly as possible. While in Mr. Bradley's there were two or three well-dressed men, I do not know their names but have seen them in this city, who appeared to be liberal with their money. These men were not drinking themselves, but the emigrants were. I saw a man, who said he was from Augusta, who appeared to be talking with the men out on the railroad track. This man said to me he was a recruiting officer, and wanted some of my help to get some of the men. I told him the police had nothing to do with business of that kind. He insinuated to me that if the men wanted liquor to aid them in getting it. I told him, no; that I did not drink myself and would not assist in procuring any for the men.

I saw no one that I knew to be connected with recruiting for this city or vicinity present during the riot, except Mr. Floyd. I do not know that Mr. Floyd is a recruiting officer. The next day I saw John W. Collins enlist Thomas Tulley, Michael Byrne, and James Higgins. They were down at Mr. Collins' recruiting office. Collins asked them if they were ready to enlist; they said they were: they were perfectly sober, and signed the papers voluntarily. During the night before they enlisted the next day, I furnished the prisoners with water and food, and had conversation with Tulley. He asked me if many of his countrymen were in the army. I told him there were. He said he came over here to fight. I asked him for what. He said it did not make a damn's difference to him whether for the North or the South; he would go where he got the most money. At 12 o'clock that night I gave Thomas Tulley five crackers and water. I gave the other prisoners water and crackers at the same time.

It is contrary to the rules of the office to refuse water or food to any prisoners whenever they call for it. We can hear the prisoners talk or shout from the cells into the police rooms, so that if any one should call they can be easily heard by the police.

After these three men signed the enlistment papers they came up to the new city building, and before they went into the Provost-Marshal's room to be mustered, they wanted to go to the police-office in the same building, and see if any others would enlist. They went down and went in with them, and Tulley tried to persuade others to enlist, but none of them did enlist.

(Signed)   JAMES H. BEWICK.

State of Maine, Cumberland, ss., April 4, 1864.

Subscribed and sworn to.
    Before me,
    (Signed)   EDWARD S. MORRIS, *Justice of the Peace.*

Inclosure 8 in No. 9.

Statement of A. Wentworth.

MY name is Alonzo Wentworth. I am one of the Deputy Marshals of the city of Portland. About 1 o'clock P.M. the 9th of March. my attention was called down to the foot of India Street, near the Grand Trunk Depot. I found when I arrived there, there was a large crowd. I found several men intoxicated. The police force arrested seven or eight men. They were fighting with each other, and with any one that came along. They were brought to the watch-house. Four of them were brought upon a team; two of the four were dead drunk and two were fighting each other. They were put into the lock-up in separate cells. I had charge of the "station-house" that night. No one had access to any of the prisoners during the night, to my knowledge, except the police. I made the records in the office. Thomas Tulley, James Higgins, Michael Moran, and Michael Byrne were brought up in the cart. One of them resisted the officers in their attempts to arrest the men. He had been drinking, but was not so drunk as the rest. I think this was Moran. About 8 o'clock the next morning Mr. Todd, the recruiting officer, came up to the office. He wanted to go in and talk with the men. I told him he could not till I made my morning return. I went into the cells and saw the prisoners. Some of them asked me what was going to be done with them. I told them they would remain there till their agent came back from Boston in the noon train. After that Mr. Collins came up and wanted to go out. He went out, came back, and said there was one that wanted to enlist. He said he would like to take him down to his "recruiting office." I told Mr. Cole to go and let him out. I think this was about half-past 9. He took him out; was gone one half or three-quarters of an hour, when Mr. Collins and the man that I had discharged wanted to go in and see the others who were in the cells. They both went into the place where the men were, stopped perhaps fifteen minutes, then came into my office. Mr. Cole soon came in; said the men were very uneasy and wanted to get out. I told him to go and let them all out. I think they were let out about half-past 10 o'clock. When they came into the office I told them they were free to go where they chose. Not one of them was enlisted while in or about the office. They had crackers and water, the same as other prisoners get. They asked for water frequently, and received it. Mr. Collins spoke to me, and wished to go in and see them in the evening. I would not permit him to, as they were too drunk. After they were once taken from the cells they were not taken back again.

(Signed)   ALONZO WENTWORTH.

State of Maine, Cumberland, ss., March 31, 1864.

Personally appeared Alonzo Wentworth, and made oath to the truth of the above statement, by him signed
    Before me,
    (Signed)   EDWARD S. MORRIS, *Justice of the Peace.*

Inclosure 9 in No. 9.

Statement of W. Foster.

MY name is William Foster; am one of the police of the city of Portland. I arrested the man who was put into the cell No. 5 of the watch-house. While we were coming from the place of arrest near the depôt of the Grand Trunk Railway to the watch-house, he said he wanted to enlist. I told him he was too drunk to enlist. This was on the afternoon of the 9th of March, and this man was one of the passengers of the steamer "Nova Scotian." I saw nothing of this man after he was put into the cell till 7 o'clock the next morning. He then asked me for water. I gave him some, and all other prisoners that were in the lock-up. After he got through drinking the water, he asked me how long they would have to stay in there. I told him they would most likely get out by 10 o'clock. I asked him if he was going to Boston to work on the railroad. He told me he should not go with that agent any further. I asked him what he thought of doing. He said he should go into the army if he got a chance. I told him that he could get as good a chance here in the army as anywhere. He asked me what the bounty was. I told him if he should enlist here, pass the surgeon, he would get 200 dollars down. I told him he would get 100 dollars or more before he left the State. He wanted to know where he could go to enlist. I told him there were plenty of recruiting officers where he could enlist. I told him as soon as he was discharged he could go down by the post-office, and there were several recruiting offices there; or if he wished me I could send to him one of his brother countrymen. He wanted me to send him, and I sent him to John W. Collins. I have not seen the man since.

(Signed)   W. FOSTER.

State of Maine, Cumberland, ss., March 31, 1864.

Personally appeared W. Foster, and made oath to the truth of the above statement, by him signed
Before me,
(Signed)   EDWARD S. MORRIS, *Justice of the Peace.*

Inclosure 10 in No. 9.

Statement of W. Irish, T. Beals, C. Williams, and M. Akers.

THE undersigned members of the police of the city of Portland testify, depose, and say, that we were present on the 9th day of March, 1864, as the police force under Deputy Marshal Alonzo Wentworth at the riot of the steerage passengers from the steam-ship "Nova Scotian," near the Grand Trunk Depôt, and we made the arrest of Thomas Tulley, Michael Bryne, James Higgins, Michael Moran, and other passengers. We further state that we carried the persons arrested into the depôt of the Grand Trunk Railway, and tried to keep them quiet there, until the train should come along to go up to the Boston depôt, that they might proceed to Boston in the train which leaves about half-past 2 o'clock P.M. We kept them there about an hour, but they were so boisterously drunk that we were obliged to carry them to the station-house for safe keeping. Four of the number were taken there on a cart.

(Signed)   WILLIAM B. IRISH.
THOMAS P. BEALS.
CHARLES H. WILLIAMS.
MUHLON AKERS.

State of Maine, Cumberland, ss., April 2, 1864.

Personally appeared the above-named William B. Irish, Thomas B. Beals, Charles H. Williams, and Muhlon Akers, and severally made oath that the above statement by them signed is true.
Before me,
(Signed)   EDWARD S. MORRIS, *Justice of the Peace.*

Inclosure 11 in No. 9.

Statement of J. Bradley, Jun.

I, JAMES BRADLEY, Junior, testify and say that I keep a public-house or hotel on the corner of India and Commercial-street, near the depôt of the Grand Trunk Railway. I was present the 9th day of March at the time of the riot of the steerage-passengers of the steam-ship "Nova Scotian." Several of the passengers came into my place at about half-past 10 o'clock in the morning, and wanted something to eat. I went up into the dining-hall. They ordered whatever they wanted. I stayed there five or ten minutes, and then went down to the first-floor again, and stayed a few minutes. The man who had the charge of the dining-hall called to me to come up and bring some silver change. I then went up to the dining-hall. They paid their bills in silver and gold, most of it English silver and gold coin. They did not call for any liquor. I have not charge of the bar. They drank with their food tea and coffee. Before the passengers came around my place between 8 and 9 o'clock A.M. a man came into my shop, and bought a demijohn of whiskey. He carried it towards the wharf where the steam-ship lay. This man was a Canadian. He told me so. I have seen him before. Don't know his name. I saw no recruiting officers or any one else pay for or order any liquor for the Irish passengers. I know all the recruiting officers. After I came down stairs the second time I saw quite a crowd in and about the bar-room. I ordered them out, and closed the doors. I asked the police officers and others to clear the side walks. I should think some of these passengers had been drinking considerably when they first came.

(Signed)   JAMES BRADLEY, Jun.

State of Maine, Cumberland, ss., April 1, 1864.

Personally appeared James Bradley, Junior, and made oath to the truth of the above statement, by him signed
Before me,
(Signed)   EDWARD S. MORRIS, *Justice of the Peace.*

Inclosure 12 in No. 9.

Statement of Lieutenant F. H. Strout.

I, LIEUTENANT F. H. STROUT, testify and say that I am on duty at the Provost-Marshal's Office in Portland. A part of my duty is to take charge of recruits after they are mustered, and see that they are properly clothed with United States' uniforms. I clothed Thomas Tulley, Michael Byrne, James Higgins, Edward Cassidy, Thomas Burke, and Michael Moran, on the 10th day of March, and Martin Hogan on the 11th. While in the clothing-room Michael Moran remarked to me that he was going out about town after he was uniformed. I told him he could not go unless a guard went with him—this is the common custom with all recruits. He asked me if I would go with him. I told him I would after I had got through with my work and had time. I went down town with him; went to W. J. Gillman's, jeweller's store. He then bought a watch and chain of Mr. Gillman. He paid 23 dollars for the watch and chain; it was a patent-lever silver-cased watch, full jewelled, and plated chain. Then I went with him to a merchant-tailor's shop. He then bought some collars, a pair of suspenders, and, I think, some other things. Then I returned with him, put him into the guard-room that adjoins the Provost-Marshal's Office, and delivered him into the charge of Serjeants Atkinson and Record, who take charge of the recruits until they are sent to the camp at 4 P.M. When I came back with him one of the other men looked at his watch, and made a remark that he would like a watch. I told him I had a watch similar to that, if not better; I would sell it to him if he wished to buy. I showed it to him; he asked me the price. I offered it for 25 dollars, watch and chain. He bought it of me, and I delivered the watch to him. I don't know his name.

(Signed)   FREDERICK H. STROUT.

State of Maine, Cumberland, ss., March 31, 1864.

Personally appeared Lieutenant F. H. Strout, and made oath that the above statement, by him signed, is true.
Before me,
(Signed)   EDWARD S. MORRIS, *Justice of the Peace.*

     F

Inclosure 13 in No. 9.

Statement of Sergeant S. D. Atkinson.

I, SAMUEL D. ATKINSON, a sergeant of the 12th Maine volunteers, testify, depose and say that I am on duty at the Provost Marshal's Office at Portland with Sergeant Record. I was on duty the 10th day of March when Tulley, Byrne, Higgins, Moran, Cassidy, and Burke were mustered in. That day there were twelve men mustered into service ; seven of them were Irishmen, the others were Yankees. One of them asked me what I would take for my watch. He commenced the conversation about the trade. I told him I would take 24 dollars for watch and chain. He paid me that sum. I do not know whether it was a Yankee or an Irishman. I went down town with one of the Irishmen who wanted to buy a watch; he bought one at Merrill's, jeweller's shop, and paid 24 dollars for watch and chain : this was just such a watch as I sold the first man. One of the other men came to me, and wanted me to go out and buy him one. I went to Merrill's and bought him a watch just like the other two, and paid the same price. I could not identify either of those men if I should see them.

(Signed)   SAMUEL D. ATKINSON.

State of Maine, Cumberland, ss., March 31, 1864.

Personally appeared Samuel D. Atkinson above named, and made oath to the truth of the statement, by him signed

Before me,

(Signed)   EDWARD S. MORRIS, *Justice of the Peace.*

Inclosure 14 in No. 9.

Statement of Sergeant A. C. Record.

I, ALEXANDER C. RECORD, a Sergeant of the 12th Maine Regiment, testify and depose and say that I am on duty at the Provost Marshal's office at Portland. My duty is to take charge of recruits who are mustered at the Provost Marshal's office. Serjeant Samuel D. Atkinson is on similar duty at the same place. I was on duty the day that Tulley, Byrne, Higgins, Moran, Cassidy and Burke were mustered the 10th day of March, and Hogan on the 11th. I sold no man any watches or jewellery, or any other things. I saw no watches or jewellery sold by any person to any of these recruits. No person to my knowledge was admitted to the room with anything to sell.

(Signed)   A. C. RECORD.

State of Maine, Cumberland, ss., March 31, 1864.

Personally appeared Alexander C. Record, and made oath to the truth of the above statement, by him signed

Before me,

(Signed)   EDWARD S. MORRIS, *Justice of the Peace.*

No. 10.

Lord Lyons to Earl Russell.—(Received May 9.)

My Lord,   *Washington, April 25, 1864.*

I HAVE the honour to transmit to you copies of two notes respecting the enlistment in the United States' army of the Irish passengers by the steam-vessel "Nova Scotian," which I have addressed to Mr. Seward, in obedience to the instructions contained in your Lordship's despatches of the 31st of March and of the 5th of April. I have also taken occasion to inclose a copy of a communication from Mr. Seward bearing the same date as my second note, and sent off before Mr. Seward received that note. It incloses a copy of a letter from the War Department stating that there seems to be no doubt that Thomas Tulley and the six other men enlisted at Portland were legally enlisted and held to service, and that therefore their discharge is not recommended.

This statement is founded on the Report of the Board of Enrolment at Portland, a copy of which was sent to me by Mr. Murray, Her Majesty's Consul at Portland, and transmitted by me to your Lordship with my despatch of the 19th instant. As I had the honour to state to your Lordship in that despatch, the Report does not appear to me to be conclusive as to the men's having been fairly dealt with; nor, indeed, do I think that, on the face of it, it quite warrants the conclusions drawn from it by the War Department. It is, moreover, founded in a great measure on the depositions of the policemen and recruiting agents, who are themselves the persons accused of having been chiefly concerned in procuring improperly the enlistment of the men. Mr. Murray bears testimony to the good faith of the members of the Board of Enrolment in conducting the inquiry, and to their earnest endeavours to obtain full and trustworthy evidence. Otherwise some exception might be taken to the selection of them to investigate the matter, for they appear to have been themselves so much concerned with the final enlistment of the men that they could hardly be acquitted of all blame if the enlistment was improper.

Taking all these circumstances into consideration, I have thought it right to address a third note to Mr. Seward, in which I have asked for a further investigation, and have urged that the men ought to be heard themselves in answer to the evidence contradicting their statement, and in which I have, moreover, earnestly requested that they may not be exposed to meet the enemy in the field until the lawfulness of their enlistment is more satisfactorily proved.

I inclose a copy of this third note, and also copies of a letter which I have received from Thomas Tulley, and of a letter which I have written to him. He is now in hospital at Washington, and has already been at the Legation. I have sent for him again; he is very intelligent, and will probably be able to throw some light on the cases of his companions, as well as on his own case.

I have, &c.
(Signed) LYONS.

Inclosure 1 in No. 10.

Lord Lyons to Mr. Seward.

Sir, *Washington, April 22, 1864.*

I HAVE the honour to inform you that I have received instructions from Her Majesty's Government to call your attention to the practices employed at Portland and Boston to induce the Irish passengers by the steam-vessel "Nova Scotian" to enlist in the United States' army, and that I am particularly directed to request that you will cause an inquiry to be made respecting the proceedings of the man named Pheany or Feeny.

Having already had the honour to address you on this matter in my notes of the 19th ultimo and 7th instant, in anticipation of the instructions of Her Majesty's Government, I will content myself on the present occasion with simply recommending it once more to the serious consideration of the Government of the United States.

I have, &c.
(Signed) LYONS.

Inclosure 2 in No. 10.

Lord Lyons to Mr. Seward.

Sir, *Washington, April 23, 1864.*

WITH a note dated the 19th ultimo I had the honour to transmit to you a copy of a despatch from Her Majesty's Consul at Portland, recounting the circumstances under which seven Irishmen, who were brought to this country by the man named Feeny or Pheany on board the steam-vessel "Nova Scotian" were induced to enter the military service of the United States. Her Majesty's Government conceive that, if the information given to Her Majesty's Consul was correct, the enlistment of these Irishmen was manifestly improper, and Her Majesty's Government have accordingly directed me to apply to the Government of the United States for their release.

Having thus acquitted myself of the duty prescribed by the instructions of Her Majesty's Government, I deem it right to revert to the applications which I made to you, in anticipation of those instructions, on the 19th ultimo and on the 7th and 8th instant, and to beg you to inform me, without delay, where the seven men now are, and what measures have been taken by the United States' Government with regard to them.

I have, &c.
(Signed) LYONS.

Inclosure 3 in No. 10.

Mr. Seward to Lord Lyons.

My Lord,　　　　　•　　　*Department of State, Washington, April* 23, 1864.
RECURRING to your communication of the 19th ultimo respecting the case of Thomas Tulley and six others alleged to have been improperly enlisted in the army of the United States, I have the honour to inclose, in reply, a copy of a communication from the War Department of the 18th instant, and to be, &c.
(Signed)　　　　WILLIAM H. SEWARD.

Inclosure 4 in No. 10.

Mr. Dana to Mr. Seward.

Sir,　　　　　　　　*War Department, Washington, April* 18, 1864.
THE Secretary of War instructs me to transmit to you the inclosed copy of the report of the Adjutant-General relative to the cases of Thomas Tulley, Michael Byrne, James Higgins, Edward Cassidy, Thomas Burke, Michael Moran, and Martin Hogan, alleged to be British subjects, and to have been improperly enlisted in the United States' army, which cases were the subject of the communication of the 19th ultimo from Lord Lyons, a copy of which accompanied your letter of the 27th of same month.
I have, &c.
(Signed)　　　　C. A. DANA, *Assistant Secretary of War.*

Inclosure 5 in No. 10.

Report.

Adjutant-General's Office, Washington, April 14, 1864.
THE Secretary of War refers communications of Lord Lyons in relation to Thomas Tulley, Michael Byrne, James Higgins, Edward Cassidy, Thomas Burke, Michael Moran, and Martin Hogan, alleged British subjects, improperly enlisted in the United States' army.
From the Report of the Board of Enrolment, Portland, Maine, it appears that these men had but just landed from an emigrant vessel, and expressed a desire to enlist, and that when enlisted, examined, and mustered, they were all sober. That some were refused examination while intoxicated, and were subsequently, when sober, presented and passed. That they voluntarily enlisted, and never objected to the performance of any duty assigned them. The examination appears to have been most impartial and thorough, and from the facts adduced, there seems no doubt that they were legally enlisted and held to service, and their discharge is therefore not recommended.
(Signed)　　　　SAMUEL BRECK, *Assistant Adjutant-General.*

Inclosure 6 in No. 10.

Lord Lyons to Mr. Seward.

Sir,　　　　　　　　　　*Washington, April* 25, 1864.
A FEW hours after I addressed to you my note of the day before yesterday's date respecting the enlistment of the seven Irish passengers who arrived at Portland in the packet "Nova Scotian," I had the honour to receive your note of the same day on the subject.
In the letter from the War Department, a copy of which is appended to your note, it is stated that it appears from a Report of the Board of Enrolment at Portland, that these men had but just landed from an emigrant vessel and expressed a desire to enlist ; that when enlisted, examined, and mustered, they were all sober, and that they voluntarily enlisted, and never objected to the performance of any duty assigned them. It is added that, from the facts adduced, there seems no doubt that they were legally enlisted, and held to service, and that, therefore, their discharge is not recommended.

The Report itself does not accompany your note, but I have received a copy of it, and copies of the affidavits annexed to it, from Her Majesty's Consul at Portland, who was courteously invited to be present at the investigation, and who bears testimony to the good faith of the members of the Board by whom it was conducted and to their earnest endeavour to obtain full and trustworthy evidence.

I have read with great attention the report and the affidavits, but I confess that they do not appear to me to show conclusively that the seven men were fairly dealt with on their arrival at Portland, or that their enlistment was truly voluntarily. I desire, therefore, to suggest that further inquiry should be made on these points.

I will, in the first place, ask you to give your attention to the observations contained in the inclosed copy of a despatch from Her Majesty's Consul at Portland, and in the second place beg you to consider that the investigation was conducted in the absence of the men themselves, and without any communication with them. I would propose that they should be themselves examined, and be afforded an opportunity of refuting the evidence given in contradiction to their original statement to Her Majesty's Consul.

You will remember that these men landed at Portland on the 9th of last month, and that two days afterwards they addressed a letter to Her Majesty's Consul at that place, stating that they had been put into prison; that they had been unable to gain their liberation or food unless they enrolled themselves in the American service, and that they had ultimately enrolled themselves through mere compulsion or privation. This statement is no doubt contradicted in essential particulars by the evidence of the policeman and the recruiting agents; but even if this evidence be admitted to be perfectly impartial, it does not, in my opinion, show conclusively that there was no foundation for the story told by the men. On the contrary, in some points it confirms their story, and it certainly seems to me to leave at least so much doubt whether the men were entirely free agents, and knew that they were entirely free agents, as to render it proper that they should be themselves heard on the subject.

I abstain from expressing here any positive opinion on the merits of the case; but I think that I have good grounds for asking for a further investigation, and for earnestly requesting that the men may not be exposed to meet the enemy of the United States in the field, until the lawfulness of their enlistment is more satisfactorily proved.

I am the more urgent in the matter because (as I had the honour to inform you in my note of the 8th instant) five of the men have already been sent to the army of the Potomac, and one of them, Thomas Tulley, who is at present in the Finley Hospital in this city, is liable to be sent at any moment to join that army in the field.

I have, &c.

(Signed)   LYONS.

Inclosure 7 in No. 10.

Thomas Tulley to Lord Lyons.

United States' Sanitary Commission, 5th Ward, Finley Hospital,
Washington, April 23, 1864.

My Lord,

WITH great submission and respect, I beg to bring myself again under your Lordship's notice, fully aware of the interest you have taken in my and companions' affair, subsequent to my presenting my petition. I perceived, in the Boston "Pilot" of the 16th instant, an article taken from the Portland "Argus," informing the public that the Board of Enrolment came to the conclusion that we received food and drink in prison, and that some of us enlisted of free will. Such assertions are, my Lord, untruthful, as my petition contains the real facts, and which I can prove on oath, and compel the parties who interfered with me to admit if legally investigated. To such article I sent a contradiction, but my letter has not yet appeared.

In the "New York Herald" of the 21st instant, I have seen the interest Sir A. Agnew (through your Lordship's kind interference) has taken in the matter; and may I therefore hope your Lordship will have the entrapped men of Portland, seven in number, and not forty-seven as stated in the "Herald," as being the number stated by Sir A. in Parliament to have been kidnapped in Portland.

My Lord, it is a sad thing to compel a man to soldier under such circumstances. The State acted contrary to every law, as why not take us before a magistrate if we broke the laws of America; but evidently they imprisoned us for the purpose of compelling our enlistment.

Hoping your Lordship will excuse my presumption, and trusting my perseverance will meet with success, I have, &c.

(Signed)   THOMAS TULLEY.

P.S.—I expect every day to be sent to the army unless something is done for my liberation.

T. T.

Inclosure 8 in No. 10.

Lord Lyons to Thomas Tulley.

Sir,   *Washington, April* 25, 1864.

I SHALL be glad if you will call at the Legation to-morrow, Tuesday. If you cannot come to-morrow, I beg you to come the next day, or the day after that. About 11 o'clock in the forenoon is the time which would suit me best, but you can come earlier or later in the day if the hospital regulations interfere with your coming at 11. Pray let me know that you have received this letter; and if there is any obstacle to your coming here again, inform me at once.

I am, &c,
(Signed)   LYONS.

No. 11.

Lord Lyons to Earl Russell.—(Received May 16.)

My Lord,   *Washington, May* 3, 1864.

THE number of British subjects who are serving in the United States' army and navy is very considerable; and complaints are constantly made to me of the practices by which the enlistment of many of them has been effected. I may say, indeed, that the most laborious and most painful and unsatisfactory part of the duties which have devolved upon this Legation, since the breaking out of the civil war, is connected with these complaints. No pains have been spared by Her Majesty's Consuls and myself in investigating them, and every effort has been made by us to obtain redress for those which have appeared to be well founded. In few cases, however, have our efforts produced any satisfactory results.

In point of form, indeed, there is little to complain of. The remonstrances addressed by me to the Secretary of State are duly acknowledged and transmitted to the War or the Navy Department. The Department orders an investigation. The recruiting agents or other officers contradict the statements made by the complainants, and affirm that the enlistments were voluntary, lawful, and correct in all particulars. I do my best to elicit the truth, and to obtain evidence. A controversial correspondence between the United States' Government and me ensues. From the nature of the case there can seldom be any evidence, except that of the recruiting officers, on one side, and the men enlisted, on the other; and commonly the United States' Government gives credence by preference to its own officers, and retains the recruits in its service.

Nor indeed is it by any means easy for me to satisfy myself as to the justness of the individual complaints that come before me. There is no doubt that some of the persons who apply to me are not entitled to British protection, that some of them have enlisted voluntarily, that some have even been in collusion with recruiting agents, and have enlisted with the intention of securing the bounties, and then obtaining their discharge by addressing this Legation as British subjects. To distinguish between cases of this kind, and those in which the complaints are well-founded, is difficult in individual instances; and it is still more difficult to obtain evidence sufficiently conclusive to induce the United States' authorities to release a recruit. But that fraud, violence, and all kinds of villany have been very generally resorted to by brokers and recruiting agents, in order to possess themselves of the immense bounties given by the Federal and State Governments for recruits, is absolutely certain.

It is particularly in the city of New York that these iniquitous practices have been prevalent. I have the honour to transmit herewith to your Lordship, a copy, taken from a newspaper, of a report made by Major-General Dix, the Military Commandant at New York, to the Chairman of the Judiciary Committee of the Senate of the State, to which are appended extracts from a report made by the General to the Secretary of War. I will give some of the statements of the General in his own words :—

" Almost every imaginable form of outrage and deception has been developed in the cases in which Mr. Clapp was Agent for the payment of bounties. . . . In some cases boys have been seduced from their homes to secure their enlistment. In others men have been drugged, and enlisted while unconscious. . . . In short there is no artifice or fraud which has not been resorted to in carrying out this system of pillage. . . . Old men and boys, and persons labouring under incurable diseases, were in numerous instances thrust into the service under this system of public plunder, alike fraudulent to the recruits and the Government. . . . The enormous sum of 400,000 dollars has been plundered by the brokers. . . . The outrages practised on recruits are too unjust to be borne, and in some cases too loathsome to be detailed. Boys have been seduced from their families, drugged, and then enlisted. Two were so sadly drugged that they died—one on his arrival at Rikers Island, and the other on the following day."

I have moreover the honour to transmit to your Lordship a copy taken from a newspaper; of a letter addressed to General Dix by General Wistar. The following are extracts from it :—

" There seems to be little doubt that many—in fact, I think I am justified in saying the most—of these unfortunate men were either deceived or kidnapped, or both, in the most scandalous and inhuman manner in New York City, where they were drugged and carried off to New Hampshire and Connecticut, mustered in, and uniformed before their consciousness was fully restored. . . . Nearly all are foreigners, mostly sailors, both ignorant of and indifferent to the objects of the war in which they thus suddenly find themselves involved. . . . Two men were shot here this morning for desertion, and over thirty more are now awaiting trial or execution."

General Dix concludes his report by saying that stringent measures have been adopted, and that this whole system of fraudulent recruiting is nearly broken up, but that a great wrong has been done to individuals in the service, and that it is impossible wholly to repair it.

Sufficient time has not elapsed to show whether the fraudulent system of recruiting has, in fact, been broken up at New York, so far as the army is concerned, by the measures taken by General Dix. I do not learn that any effectual steps have been taken to put a stop to the practices, similar in their nature and equal in their iniquity, which have been resorted to by brokers and crimps at New York to obtain sailors for the United States' navy.

I ought, perhaps, to say that in the only two instances in which it has come to my knowledge that a British subject has been condemned to death for desertion from the United States' army, I have succeeded in preventing the execution of the sentence. In one case the man was ultimately released from arrest, and discharged altogether from the army. In the other, the evidence that the prisoner had been improperly enlisted did not appear to be conclusive, and I was unable to obtain his discharge from the army, but the sentence of death was, nevertheless, commuted to imprisonment.

I refrain, on the present occasion, from transmitting to your Lordship any portion of the voluminous correspondence which I have had with Her Majesty's Consuls and with the United States' Government on the cases of individual British subjects who have complained of being improperly enlisted. In justice, however, to Mr. Archibald, Her Majesty's Consul at New York, in whose district by far the greater number of the cases have occurred, and on whom they have imposed no ordinary amount of labour and anxiety, I feel bound to say at once that the correspondence shows that he has been indefatigable in his endeavours to rescue Her Majesty's subjects from the villainous practices of the recruiting agents.

I have, &c.

(Signed)   LYONS.

Inclosure 1 in No. 11.

Extract from the " New York Times" of April 16, 1864.

FRAUDS ON RECRUITS.—THE LAFAYETTE HALL BOUNTY BROKERS. — Hawley D. Clapp, recognized as the head and front here of bounty brokers, was arrested and sent to Fort Lafayette, where he yet remains. He addressed some time since an appeal to the Legislature for relief. The matter was referred to the Judiciary Committee, who applied to General Dix, who caused the arrest, for information on the subject. The following is the General's reply :—

"Hon. Chas. J. Folger, Chairman of the Senate Judiciary Committee.

" *Head-Quarters Department of the East, New York City,*
"Dear Sir, " *April* 11, 1864.
" Your note of the 9th instant was received to-day, and it affords me pleasure to furnish you with the facts and circumstances attending the arrest and imprisonment of Hawley D. Clapp.

" When your note came to hand I was completing a report to the Secretary of War (a copy of which, with accompanying papers, I inclose), giving a detailed statement of the atrocious frauds committed upon recruits in this city, and particularly at Lafayette Hall, where Mr. Clapp was the principal bounty broker—one of a class of agents who were brought into existence by the system adopted by the Committee of the Board of Supervisors, for procuring substitutes, whose services were entirely unnecessary, and whose principal vocation, either by their own direct action or through confederates, was to cheat men entering the service out of their bounties. The Committee, when the frauds had become too palpable and too extensive to be borne, obviated the evil, as far as they could, by the adoption of proper precautions, but not until a military order had been issued requiring the full amount of bounty to be paid to the recruit.

" My report to the Secretary of War enters into a full detail of those transactions, alike disgraceful to those who were concerned in them and to the community in the bosom of which they occurred. Mr. Clapp received from the Committee of the Supervisors the bounties for a large number of recruits (300 dollars for each), who, as shown by testimony satisfactory to me, were cheated out of the greater part of it, by him, or the parties confederated with him in the business. As the money was paid into his hands, I consider him responsible for it ; and I have deemed it my duty, whenever a clear case of fraud was made out, to see the soldier redressed, if possible.

" It is only by the summary process of a military arrest that these fraudulent transactions can be reached. If they are brought into the civil courts, all remedy is hopeless. The recruits are the only witnesses, and the exigencies of the country will not permit them to be kept from the field.

" The only alternatives, therefore, were to allow these stupendous frauds to go unredressed, to let patriotic men who are offering their lives on the altar of their country be robbed of the provisions which their fellow-citizens have made for their families, and to suffer the plunderers to escape with their ill-gotten gains, or to take, as I have done, some of the principal agents in these frauds into custody, to be held till they make restitution.

" The amounts of which recruits were defrauded at Lafayette Hall, where and while Mr. Clapp was chief broker, cannot fall short of 400,000 dollars. I have succeeded in recovering about 20,000 dollars, and am not without hopes of adding largely to this amount.

" I am fully aware of the responsibility I have taken in these cases, and that the exercise of the power of arrest is only warranted by the circumstances in which the country is placed, and the special facts which my report to the Secretary of War discloses. It has been exerted in a few cases only, and with the confident assurance in each, that I should be sustained by the Government and by the public judgment.

" Although it is technically true, as Mr. Clapp states in his petition to the Legislature, that ' he has not held at any time office under the Government, or had any contracts with the Government' itself, he stood in his capacity as bounty broker in a relation to the military service of which he seems to appreciate neither the scope nor the force.

" Lafayette Hall, in which his agency was transacted, was occupied for military purposes. It was guarded by sentinels, and the acts for which he was arrested were performed within the lines. It was for all essential purposes a camp, and he was within it, furnished with office room, and other conveniences for himself and clerks, and engaged in paying recruits their bounties as chief broker, under an appointment, not directly from the Government, but from General Spinola, the Commanding officer. He was personally engaged in services of a strictly military character, and standing in a much nearer relation to the Government than many classes of camp followers and retainers, who are by act of Congress subject to martial law. My own judgment is strongly inclined to the conclusion that he may be tried by court-martial, and if he has not been brought before one ere this, one chief reason is, that I desired to satisfy myself by consulting the course of proceedings in analogous cases, that I should not err in holding him to account before such a tribunal for the acts with which he is charged.

"Almost every imaginable form of outrage and deception has been developed in the cases in which Mr. Clapp was agent for the payment of bounties. Men, both white and coloured, were offered employment as teamsters, wagon-masters and officers' servants, receiving from 20 to 50 dollars as 'pay in advance,' and finding themselves enlisted as private soldiers, while Mr. Clapp received from 300 dollars to 315 dollars in each case. With what confederates the money was divided, he and they only can tell.

"I have considered it enough that it was received by him, and not paid to the recruits who were entitled to it. In some cases boys have been seduced from their homes to secure their enlistment. In others men have been drugged and enlisted while unconscious. In others they have promised furloughs, and where the full bounty was not paid, they have been told that they would receive the balance as soon as they should arrive at Riker's Island. In short, there is no artifice or fraud which has not been resorted to in carrying out this system of pillage.

"In one case reported to these head-quarters by Mr. Supervisor Blunt, Mr. Clapp was compelled to make restitution, and his conduct was such that he was not allowed to transact business with the Supervisors in his own name, but continued it in the name of other parties.

"I feel convinced that no class of men would be likely to take part in these outrages upon our gallant soldiers, or sympathize with the perpetrators, unless they cherished a secret sympathy with those who are endeavouring by force of arms to overthrow and destroy the government of their country.

"Mr. Clapp has been treated since his confinement with a leniency he does not deserve. He has had the same food as the men whom he has defrauded, and is much more comfortably lodged and sheltered. His Counsel has been permitted to hold two private interviews with him, a privilege not usually granted to inmates of Fort Lafayette. I have indulged the hope that he would consent to disclose the names of others more prominent than himself, who are believed to have participated in his fraudulent gains. He is not held for this purpose alone, but with the further view to compel complete restitution to those he has wronged, when the extent of the frauds in which he is implicated shall be ascertained, and also punished, and also for trial and punishment if it shall be decided that he is amenable to a military court. It has afforded me pleasure to comply with the request of your Committee, and I earnestly hope that the disclosures I have made may lead to some legislative provisions to secure to recuits the bounties intended to be paid to them. I take the liberty of stating that in some instances the authorities of towns have of the 300 dollars raised for bounties, voted 100 dollars to the recruit, and 200 dollars to the broker or runner; a temptation to cupidity which has led to every species of unfairness, deception, and fraud.

"I am satisfied that the Legislature could never have anticipated so gross a wrong to recruits, to taxpayers, and the public service, and that suitable restraints will be imposed upon local authorities.

"I have the honour also to transmit herewith a certified copy of the order under which Mr. Clapp was sent to Fort Lafayetté by Brigadier-Generel Stannard, commanding New York City and harbour.

"I am, &c.

(Signed) "JNO. A. DIX, *Major-General.*"

Report of General Dix to the Secretary of War.

(Extract.)

"When I was informed that recruits were defrauded of their bounties at Lafayette Hall, I sent for General Spinola, and communicated to him the information I had received. He denied the truth of the statements, and assured me that the recruiting regulations were fully complied with; that no man was enlisted without being fully apprised of the nature of the service in which he was engaging; that no recruit was defrauded of his

G

bounty ; and that where a less sum than that allowed by the county was paid, it was always by voluntary and amicable agreement.

* * * * * * * *

" Old men and boys, and persons labouring under incurable diseases, were in numerous instances thrust into the service under this system of public plunder, alike fraudulent to the recruits and the Government.

" I sent for General Spinola several times, and always received from him the assurance that all was fairly conducted by the officers at Lafayette Hall. The evidence to the contrary became so conclusive that I directed Lieutenant Cole and the contract surgeon, Dr. Kerrigan, to be arrested. They have since been tried ; the former dismissed the service, and the latter, who holds no military commission, disqualified for future employment.

" In my interviews with General Spinola I objected to the whole system of brokerage, as calculated rather to prevent rather than promote enlistments.

" General Spinola defended the system of brokerage, and said that without it 'the Government could get no recruits.' The result has been precisely the reverse. The bounty in the payment of which these frauds have been committed is that paid by the city of New York, amounting to 300 dollars per man, with a fee of 15 dollars per man to the person presenting the recruit. About 2,000 men were recruited by General Spinola. The average amount of bounty paid to them, as he stated in an explanation volunteered to Major Halpine, was about 100 dollars per man. The other 200 dollars per man has been plundered by the brokers and their coadjutors. Thus 200,000 dollars have been paid to the recruits, and the enormous sum of 400,000 dollars have been plundered by the brokers. It is one of the most stupendous frauds ever committed in this country ; it has gone for the most part into the hands of public plunderers, some of whom are of notoriously infamous character, and one of whom is known to be a convict who has been an inmate of the State prison.

" Among the men engaged in these frauds was Theodore Allen, of whom the Superintendent of Police says that his reputation with the force is that of a thief. He swears that he was well known to Mr. Brennan, the Comptroller, and the Supervisors, and that, through the friendship of the former, and the approval of the Supervisors, enlistment blanks, countersigned by one of the Supervisors' Committee, were given by the Superintendent in person to him. This man may be regarded in his leading characteristics, portrayed by the Superintendent of Police, as a type of the group of the depredators engaged in plundering recruits.

* * * * * * * *

" I have recovered and paid over to parties thus defrauded about 20,000 dollars, and hope to secure a much larger amount.

" The outrages practised on recruits are too unjust to be borne, and in some cases too loathsome to be detailed. Boys have been seduced from their families, drugged, and then enlisted. Two were so sadly drugged that they died ; one on his arrival at Riker's Island, and the other the following day.

" Stringent measures have been adopted, and this whole system of fraudulent recruiting is nearly broken up ; but a great wrong has been done to individuals in the service, and it is impossible wholly to repair it."

Inclosure 2 in No. 11.

Extract from the " New York Herald" of April 20, 1864.

IMPORTANT LETTER FROM GENERAL WISTAR.—VICTIMS OF THE BOUNTY SWINDLERS DESERTING IN LARGE NUMBERS.—EVILS OF THE PLUNDERING SYSTEM ON OUR ARMIES IN THE FIELD, &c.

Head-Quarters, United States' Forces, Yorktown,
General, *Virginia, April 15, 1864.*

AN extended spirit of desertion prevailing among the recruits recently received from the North, in some of the regiments in my command, has led me to make some inquiries resulting in apparently well-authenticated information, which I beg respectfully to communicate to you in this unofficial manner, deeming it required by humanity, no less than by our common desire to benefit the service.

There seems to be little doubt that many, in fact I think I am justified in saying the most, of these unfortunate men were either deceived or kidnapped, or both, in the most scandalous and inhuman manner, in New York city, where they were drugged and carried off to New Hampshire and Connecticut, mustered in and uniformed before their consciousness was fully restored.

Even their bounty was obtained by the parties who were instrumental in these nefarious transactions, and the poor wretches find themselves, on returning to their senses, mustered soldiers, without any pecuniary benefit. Nearly all are foreigners, mostly sailors, both ignorant of and indifferent to the objects of the war in which they thus suddenly find themselves involved.

Two men were shot here this morning for desertion, and over thirty more are now awaiting trial or execution.

These examples are essential, as we all understand ; but it occurred to me, General, that you would pardon me for thus calling your attention to the greater crime committed in New York, of kidnapping these men into positions where, to their ignorance, desertion must seem like a vindication of their own rights and liberty.

Believe me, &c.

(Signed)   J. J. WISTAR.

To Major-General John A. Dix, New York City.

No. 12.

Earl Russell to Lord Lyons.

My Lord,   *Foreign Office, May 19*, 1864.

YOU will endeavour to impress on Mr. Seward in friendly communication the duty of putting an end to the imprisonment of British subjects, whose sole offence consists in their being on board vessels which have attempted to run the blockade. You will point out to Mr. Seward that while the Government of Great Britain perform their obligations as a neutral to a belligerent, the Government of the United States are bound to perform their corresponding obligations as a belligerent towards a neutral.

The practice of drugging men in order to procure their services in the United States' army and navy is an abuse of the most odious description, and in the case of the British subjects in question justifies the strongest remonstrances.

But I trust that Mr. Seward, unwilling to excite feelings of just indignation in this country, will put an end to both the abuses to which I have instructed you thus to call his attention.

I am, &c.

(Signed)   RUSSELL.

No. 13.

Lord Lyons to Earl Russell.—(Received May 24.)

My Lord,   *Washington, May 9,* 1864.

WITH reference to my despatch of the 25th ultimo, and to the previous correspondence on the subject of the Irish passengers by the packet " Nova Scotian " who were enlisted in the United States' army, I have the honour to transmit to your Lordship herewith copies of further papers relating to the same subject.

Your Lordship will perceive that Mr. Seward has communicated to me information from the War Department, to the effect that the cases of Thomas Tulley and his five companions are now in process of investigation, and that a prominent officer implicated in the alleged improper enlistments will be brought to trial.

I have written to Mr. Seward to repeat the expression of my hope that the men themselves will be heard in their own cause, and that due weight will be given to their testimony. I have also reiterated my urgent request that measures may be taken to remove those of the men who had been sent to the army of the Potomac from the scene of hostilities.

Tulley has been twice at the Legation ; the second time he was sent by the United States' authorities in consequence of an application from me. Among the inclosures in this despatch is a statement made by him, which distinctly contradicts in many important particulars the evidence of the policemen and recruiting agents at Portland. He has now been removed to a hospital further north. I did not receive the letter in which he informed me that he was about to be removed, in time to interpose with the United States' authorities in order to keep him here. I should however have had

G 2

no desire to do so. On the contrary, I am glad that he should be sent further from the theatre of war, and thus be less likely to be suddenly placed in the ranks of the army in the field.

I have, &c.
(Signed)   LYONS.

Inclosure 1 in No. 13.

Consul Lousada to Lord Lyons.

My Lord,   *Boston, April 18, 1864.*

I HAVE the honour to acknowledge your Lordship's despatch of the 7th instant, and to report that James Traynor, one of the Irishmen brought over by Finney, presented himself at the office to-day in military costume, and stated that he was drunk when he enlisted, and wanted me to assist him in obtaining his release. He had received thirty dollars, and believed he was to have more when the company left for active service.

His Company is Letter I, 59th Massachusetts, and I understand that the regiment goes to Annapolis on Thursday.

In answer to my questions, he said that neither himself nor his comrades had any idea of enlisting when they entrusted themselves to Finney, but really thought they were coming to work here on high wages.

I have, &c.
(Signed)   F. LOUSADA.

Inclosure 2 in No. 13.

Lord Lyons to Mr. Seward.

Sir,   *Washington, April 27, 1864.*

WITH reference to my note of the 22nd instant, I have the honour to call your attention to the inclosed copy of a despatch from Her Majesty's Consul at Boston reporting a statement made by James Traynor, one of the Irishmen brought over to this country in the steamer " Nova Scotian," respecting the circumstances under which he enlisted in the United States' military service.

I beg you to cause this case to be investigated in order that the man may be discharged, if it shall appear that he did not enlist of his own free will, and with a full knowledge of what he was doing.

I have, &c.
(Signed)   LYONS.

Inclosure 3 in No. 13.

Mr. Seward to Lord Lyons.

My Lord,   *Department of State, Washington, April 30, 1864.*

I HAVE the honour to acknowledge the receipt of your note of the 27th instant, relating to James Traynor, a passenger to this country by the " Nova Scotian," and who is represented to have been improperly enlisted in the military service. In reply I have the honour to inform your Lordship that I have referred the case to the War Department.

I have, &c.
(Signed)   WILLIAM H. SEWARD.

Inclosure 4 in No. 13.

Thomas Tulley to Lord Lyons.

My Lord,   *5th Ward, Finley Hospital, Washington, April 26, 1864.*

I HAVE the honour to acknowledge the receipt of your communication bearing the date of the 24th instant, and I sincerely regret that it is not in my power to go to the Embassy this day, but the doctor in charge of my ward has promised me a pass to-morrow; but should anything prevent my going there, I will be with your Lordship the following day, please God, and as soon as I can after 11 o'clock A.M.

Wishing your Lordship every happiness, I have, &c.

(Signed)   THOMAS TULLEY.

Inclosure 5 in No. 13.

Thomas Tulley to Lord Lyons.

My Lord,   *5th Ward, Finley Hospital, Washington, April 27, 1864.*
I HAD the honour of informing you yesterday, by letter, that I would be with you
this day or to-morrow, but my anticipations of such a liberty are destroyed, as the doctor
this morning refused me permission to visit your residence, and has even taken my clothes
away from me, as he alleges, for a breach of military regulations. Now, my Lord, this
again operates against my attempt at freedom from the institution I have been compelled
to become a member of. As my rejoicement was intense on receiving your letter, and
now, my Lord, I am prevented from availing myself of the honour of an interview with
your Lordship, my mind urges me to speak more vindictively, but refrain from doing so
through respect for your Lordship, as Representative of the country where true and real
liberty is only to be found.
Under the circumstances, I hope my non-attendance will not operate against me, and
that, if necessary, you get an order from some Government official for my appearance
before you, and if you do not require me, I beseech your Lordship to intimate to me your
Lordship's opinion of the matter.

I have, &c.
(Signed)   THOMAS TULLEY.

P.S.—Pursuant to your Lordship's injunctions I would have written you thus on
receipt of your letter, were it not for the promise made by an American officer, which he
subsequently deviated from.
I fear they will send me from here immediately if they suspect my movements.

T. T.

Inclosure 6 in No. 13.

Lord Lyons to Mr. Seward.

Sir,   *Washington, April 27, 1864.*
WITH reference to my note of the 25th instant, respecting Thomas Tulley, a British
subject, now an inmate of the Finley Hospital, Washington, I have the honour to state
that, as I wish to communicate with this person, I should be much obliged if directions
could be given either that he may be sent to this Legation from the hospital to speak to
me, or that a member of the Legation may be admitted to visit him, as may be deemed
most convenient.

I have, &c.
(Signed)   LYONS.

Inclosure 7 in No. 13.

Mr. Seward to Lord Lyons.

My Lord,   *Department of State, Washington, April 27, 1864.*
I HAVE the honour to acknowledge the receipt of your notes of the respective
dates of the 22nd, 23rd, and 25th instant, relative to the cases of Thomas Tulley and
six other persons, alleged to be British subjects, and to have been improperly enlisted in
the army of the United States; and, in reply, to inform your Lordship that the matter has
again been submitted to the Secretary of War with a view to a re-examination.

I have, &c.
(Signed)   WILLIAM H. SEWARD.

Inclosure 8 in No. 13.

Statement of Thomas Tulley.

Collins' Evidence.—I told Collins I would enlist if let out of prison; but I said so
thinking I would get my liberty, although I had no intention of it. On such assertion I
was permitted to leave my cell, but on going out I was presented the enlistment papers
by the officers of the prison, but which I refused to sign, when I was again locked-up.

When I was let out the second time Collins was ordered to bring me back unless, I enlisted, and that, in fact, he was responsible for me. Collins brought me to his office, and without any questions made out my papers, to which I partly again objected, but fearing my cell I signed the papers. Tulley suggested that he would like to see the British Consul ; to which Collins replied, There is no use in your doing so, he (meaning Mr. Murray) is as much an American as any man in Portland. This occurred either in my cell or on my way to the recruiting depôt, and previous to my enlistment.

Respecting Byrne, his desire for joining the United States' army was principally to share the same fate as Tulley and Higgins.

Had the police not been watching Tulley and his companions, he would have made his escape to the British Consul.

Harrison Cole, Police Officer.—This man states falsely when he says that on the morning of the 10th he gave Tulley, &c., crackers. as he did no such thing, although they were frequently demanded, or something in the shape of food, which was denied. Probably I am the person referred to as having been released, and doing my utmost to coerce the others to enlist. If so, such is false, as I was released and locked up again, and instead of coercing them I did my endeavours to prevent them.

No police officer told us going out of prison with Collins that we could do as we choose ; but, on the contrary, one in authority told Collins to bring us back unless we enlisted.

James Berrick.—This man swears he served us with food, which is false, as he did not give Tulley or any of his companions five (or any) crackers at any time, but he gave them some water after their lungs had been strained shouting for it.

On the night of the 9th, Tulley might have expressed himself as stated, but he positively denies having uttered such words, or expressed himself in the manner sworn to on his becoming sober next morning, 10th instant, with regard to his fighting for North or South.

Alonzo Wentworth.—It is not true as stated in affidavit that we received crackers, nor is it true what he told us that we could go where we choose ; on the contrary, this is, I think, the person who told Collins unless we enlisted we were to be brought back to cells.

William Foster.—Everything stated in this affidavit respecting Tulley, who was in cell No. 5, is false, as he never had such a discourse with any policeman, although something similar might have occurred in Tulley's insobriety.

Board of Enrolment.—Their belief in our sobriety when enlisting is correct. We enlisted to escape starvation, not voluntarily.

As far as I have written about myself Byrne and Higgins I can support on oath ; but as far as I am concerned respecting Moran, Cassidy, and Burke, I know no more than that they were imprisoned with me, went out of prison before I did, and became soldiers under the circumstances which compelled myself, as I believe.

The man Hogan was at his liberty, but when I saw him brought in as a soldier he was raging with drink, but whether he received the drink before or after his enlistment I don't know.

Notwithstanding all the affidavits made affirming that food was supplied, and that no compulsion was in question, Tulley, Higgins, and Byrne can make an affidavit denying the entire.

April 29, 1864.

(Signed)   THOMAS TULLEY, 20th *Maine Regiment*,
At present at No. 5 Ward, Finley Hospital, Washington.

Inclosure 9 in No. 13.

Michael Byrne and four others to Lord Lyons.

.. My Lord,   *Rappahannock Station, April* 26, 1864.

I WRITE to you in hopes of your seeking after me and my comrades who have been villainously kidnapped into the United States' army. We landed on the 9th day of March, and we were all welcomed to this country, and told us all we were a fine lot of men, and some of the agents represented themselves as Irishmen, and brought some of us to a public-house, and said to drink plenty at their expense, as they knew that we had no money, and that they expected us over a day or two sooner, but to never mind that—they should be as friends to us all, so we did drink a little. But after the second drink of the liquor, we all thought that the house was turning upside down ; so we knew no more until we all were in the police-house in Portland, and in some part of the evening some of those agents came to us, and asked if we would join the army, and we one and all told them that we would not do any such thing. So next morning they came to us again and wanted us to enlist, and we told them we would not, and also the police said we would have to stop for sixty days if we would not enlist, and we said to let us go before the magistrate or any of the authorities in the town, and the police said we would not be brought before no one, and we should have to stop where we were, if not to enlist. We asked for a drink of water, and they told us likewise that neither a drink nor nothing to eat we would be allowed to get for the sixty days. So it is for a drink of water and threatened to be starved, that we had to sign our names, but then refused to go when we got a drink of water, but they told us if we refused to do what they compelled us to do, that they would blow out our brains; so we said if we were in a strange country that we would get a little fair play, and they said a man's life would be taken, and for 23 dollars be let free, so that frightened us all. The doctor would not pass any of us. So we were sent willing or not. I refused to take 173 dollars, and I came away from Portland, and I got none of it as yet, and as for that or any of the others I don't want it at all. I and my comrades wants is our liberty. My Lord, that man Finney came to Berry camp, Portland, and maybe stopped from us 100 dollars for kidnapping us to this country. And, my Lord, if that is not plain to be seeing that this Government sent this Finney to Ireland to kidnap us to America. For which I hope the English Government will take it up. We have served in India and all Her Majesty's stations on foreign places, and I hope they may want us again in a just cause, as this is. And, my Lord, I am going to write to the War Department of England, and to state the whole case. And also Mr. Murray, the English Consul, got 100 dollars from Colonel Murrell of the 17th Maine Volunteer regiment, commanding Camp at Berry, Portland. From Thomas Burk, 20th Western (?) Virginia regiment, and when he wrote to Mr. Murray about it and about the bounty-money, he would not send a word in answer. So our real opinion is that he is bribed by the people of Portland, and the War Department and the English Crown shall know of all this.

The men that came with us from Dublin and went to Boston and snapped up by the enlisting agents was discharged by the people, and the British Consul of Boston by looking after them. So my Lord, we do now appeal to you for to get us our liberty and to go home again to our wives and family that is expecting us to do something for them. But when we were robbed out of all we had, what could we do, my Lord? We do humbly beg of you to send a letter to us as soon as possible, and seek after our rights.

We are, &c.

(Signed)   MICHAEL BYRNE,
THOMAS BURKE,
EDWARD CASSIDY,
JAMES HIGGINS,
MICHAEL HORAN,

D Company 20th Maine Volunteer Regiment, Rappahannock Station.

Inclosure 10 in No. 13.

Lord Lyons to Michael Byrne and four others.

Gentlemen,   *Washington, April 29, 1864.*
IN reply to your letter which I received this morning, I have to inform you that Her Majesty's Consul at Portland, Maine, did all he could in your behalf, and duly reported the case to me. I have since been in communication with the United States' Government, and am now doing all in my power to have justice done to you.

I am, &c.
(Signed)   LYONS.

Inclosure 11 in No. 13.

Mr. Seward to Lord Lyons.

My Lord,   *Department of State, Washington, April 30, 1864.*
I HAVE the honour to acknowledge the receipt of your note of the 27th instant, relating to Thomas Tulley, an inmate of Finley Hospital, and, in reply, to inform your Lordship that Brigadier-General Martindale has been instructed to send Tulley to Her Majesty's Legation at 12 o'clock meridian on Monday next.

I have, &c.
(Signed)   WILLIAM H. SEWARD.

Inclosure 12 in No. 13.

Mr. Seward to Lord Lyons.

My Lord, ━ ▓▓▓▓   *Department of State, Washington, May* 4, 1864.
RECURRING to your notes of the 22nd, 23rd, and 25th ultimo, which relate to the
cases of Thomas Tulley and six other Irishmen, passengers on the steamer "Nova Scotian,"
who were alleged to have been improperly enlisted into the United States' army, I have
the honour to inclose, in reply, a copy of a letter of the 3rd instant, from the War Department, on the subject, and to be, &c.

(Signed)   WILLIAM H. SEWARD.

Inclosure 13 in No. 13.

Brigadier-General Canby to Mr. Seward.

Sir,   *War Department, Washington, May* 3, 1864.
THE Secretary of War instructs me to acknowledge the receipt of your letter of the
12th ultimo, respecting the cases of Thomas Tulley and six other British subjects, and
inviting attention to the copy of two notes of the respective dates of the 22nd and 25th
ultimo, from Lord Lyons, and suggesting re-examination of these cases.
In reply, the Secretary instructs me to advise you that they are now in process of
investigation, and that a prominent officer implicated in these alleged improper enlistments
will be brought to trial, the result of which will be communicated to you as soon as reported
to the Department.

I have, &c.
(Signed)   ED. R. S. CANBY.

Inclosure 14 in No. 13.

Thomas Tulley to Lord Lyons.

My Lord,   *5th Ward, Finley Hospital, Washington, May* 5, 1864.
I BEG leave most respectfully to inform you that my name has been sent in to the
Medical Department, United States' Army, for transfer to some hospital northwards, but to
what place I am not aware of; and we start on to-morrow (Friday). I have been warned
so suddenly I could not acquaint you sooner. Should anything interfere which will prevent
my going I will inform you; but if I go, on my arrival at my destination I will again
write to your Lordship, unless you wish to detain me in Washington, and which, no doubt,
you can should you think it necessary. The other men are in D Company, 20th Maine
Regiment. It is a matter of great misfortune to me to be sent away so suddenly, and
probably the matter so near investigation; still I am certain your Lordship will leave
nothing undone for my benefit and the other men, all of whom have families in
Ireland.

I have, &c.
(Signed)   THOMAS TULLEY.

Inclosure 15 in No. 13.

Lord Lyons to Mr. Seward.

Sir,   *Washington, May* 8, 1864.
I HAVE the honour to acknowledge the receipt of the note dated the 4th instant,
with which you have been so good as to transmit to me a copy of a letter from the War
Department, stating that the cases of Thomas Tulley and the six other British subjects
who are represented to have been improperly enlisted at Portland are now in process of
investigation, and that a prominent officer implicated in these alleged improper enlistments
will be brought to trial.
It would be satisfactory to me to know the name of the place at which the fresh
investigation is in progress, and to be informed that my request that the men themselves
may be heard in their own cause has been attended to.
Thomas Tulley has been questioned at this Legation, and he very positively contradicts

much of the evidence of the policemen and recruiting agents, and makes statements which confirm my opinion that no satisfactory conclusion respecting the cases can be arrived at, unless his evidence and that of his companions be taken in full and allowed due weight.

I trust also that the cass of Michael Traynor (another of the Irish passengers by the " Nova Scotian "), whose enlistment formed the subject of my note to you of the 27th ultimo, will not be omitted in the investigation.

I learn that Tulley himself has been transferred from the Finley Hospital to some hospital farther north, and I am desirous of knowing where he now is. I am also anxious to learn what has become of Martin Hogan, whom I have been unable to trace. But most of all I desire to be assured that measures have been taken to give effect to the earnest request which I made that none of these men might be exposed to meet the enemy in the field until the lawfulness of their enlisting was satisfactorily proved. Five of them, Michael Byrne, James Higgins, Edward Cassidy, Thomas Burke, and Michael Horan were so lately as on the 26th of last month serving with the army of the Potomac in Company D of the 20th Regiment of Maine Volunteers. You will easily understand the anxiety with which I wait to be informed that they have been removed from the theatre of war, and exempted from actual service pending the investigation of the lawfulness of their enlistment.

I have, &c.

(Signed)   LYONS.

No. 14.

Earl Russell to Lord Lyons.

My Lord,   *Foreign Office, May* 27, 1864.

HER Majesty's Government have considered, in communication with the Law Advisers of the Crown, your Lordship's despatches of the 14th of March and 19th of April, relative to the case of the Irishmen recently enlisted at Portland and Boston for service in the United States' army; and I have to state to you that it appears to Her Majesty's Government to be clear from these papers, and from the reports on the same subject which have been received from Her Majesty's Consuls at those ports, that no doubt can be entertained that the enlistment of these Irishmen was the result of a fraudulent scheme, contrived and executed in disregard of the laws and neutral rights of Great Britain.

Her Majesty's Government consider that the men enlisted at Portland were induced, in evident bad faith and under false pretences, to leave their own country for the purpose of obtaining employment which was not really ready for them on their arrival in the United States; that on landing at Portland they were designedly plied with drink, and that they were then dealt with in a manner which (although it might be the legal consequence of their disordered condition) made it natural and almost inevitable that they should easily yield to the persuasions of the recruiting officers, who were on the look-out for them, and who obtained access to them while in confinement, by the aid of the police authorities.

Her Majesty's Government are of opinion that, notwithstanding the report made by the Provost-Marshal and the Board of Enrolment at Portland, the facts of the case are sufficient to warrant your Lordship in pressing your application to the United States' Government for the discharge of these men.

As between one Government and another the testimony of Berwick and Bradley, annexed to the report, and very properly referred to by Mr. Consul Murray, ought to suffice for this application. The latter proves that some one (name unknown) carried a large quantity of whiskey to the wharf where the ship lay with the emigrants. It is clear that this man must have been concerned for the recruiting officers, whether they directly sanctioned the particular act or not. The former proves that at the liquor stores there were "well dressed men" who were "liberal with their money," not drinking themselves, but supplying drink to these unfortunate men, and who requested the police to aid them in enlisting the men, and giving them drink. Her Majesty's Government consider that upon this evidence and upon the general circumstances of the case, your Lordship might reasonably expect to obtain the release of these men.

The case of the men landed from the " Nova Scotian " at Portland, and afterwards transferred to Boston, although not similar in its particular circumstances, should be dealt with on the same principles.

I am, &c.

(Signed)   RUSSELL.

My Lord,   *Washington, May 23,* 1864.

SINCE I first became acquainted two months ago with the circumstances under which some of the Irish passengers on board the "Nova Scotian" had been enlisted in the United States' army at Portland, I have never ceased to urge the United States' Government to take measures to prevent their being brought into collision with the enemy pending the investigation of the lawfulness of their enlistment. The copies of notes to Mr. Seward which have been inclosed in my despatches to your Lordship will have shown your Lordship how often I have insisted upon this in writing. I have pressed it still oftener and still more urgently in verbal communications. My endeavours have, however, been of no avail. One of the men called at the Legation the day before yesterday. He had been badly wounded in the head, and sent back from the army to a hospital here. Another of the men had, he said, been wounded; a third was reported to be killed; three others, when he last saw them, were advancing against the enemy under a heavy musketry fire.

I went immediately to Mr. Seward, and after telling him what had occurred, spoke to him with some warmth of the neglect with which my representations had been treated, and begged him to do something at once to remove any of the men who might still be alive from the scene of hostilities.

Mr. Seward said it was certainly very unfortunate that the men should have been wounded, but that he supposed that as they had been formally enlisted in the service of the United States, the presumption was that their enlistment was valid and lawful, and that there could be no complaint against their being made to serve until the contrary was proved.

I said that considering all we knew of the practices which had been employed to obtain recruits for the army, I really thought that in cases which were on the face of them doubtful, it would not be too much to say that the presumption was the other way. But however this might be, I must, I said, urge once more my often repeated request. I did not obtain anything more from Mr. Seward than the usual formal assurance that he would communicate my wishes to the War Department. On my return home I wrote a note to him reiterating my request.

I have the honour to inclose a copy of a statement taken down in writing from the mouth of Michael Byrne, the wounded man who came to the Legation, and copies of correspondence with Mr. Seward and Thomas Tulley.

I have, &c.
(Signed)   LYONS.

Inclosure 1 in No. 15.

Statement of Michael Byrne.

British Legation, Washington, May 21, 1864.

MICHAEL BYRNE states that he, Thomas Burke, James Higgins, Michael Moran, Martin Hogan, and Edward Cassidy were sent from Portland to join the 20th Regiment of Maine Volunteers at Rappahannock Station on Monday the 14th of March, and that they joined that regiment on the following Friday. That on the 1st instant they marched with the regiment to the Wilderness Tavern, and encamped there on the night of the 4th. That they knew they would meet the enemy, but were afraid to make any objections as they were told if they did do so they would have their brains blown out. That he was wounded on the 5th instant on the right temple by a minie ball, and went on Sunday the 8th to Fredericksburgh, whence on Wednesday the 11th instant he was sent to Carver's Hospital, Washington, where he arrived on the same afternoon, and still is under medical treatment. That he has heard that Michael Moran was killed on the 5th instant at the Wilderness, but does not know it for certain. That Edward Cassidy was wounded in the right thumb whilst carrying him (Michael Byrne) when wounded to the rear; that Cassidy was sent from Fredericksburgh to the Brick Hospital, Washington, on Wednesday the 11th instant. That he last saw Thomas Burke, James Higgins, and Martin Hogan on the 5th of May at the Wilderness advancing under a heavy musketry fire, but that since he was wounded he has not seen or heard anything of them.

Inclosure 2 in No. 15.

Mr. Seward to Lord Lyons.

My Lord,   *Department of State, Washington, May 10, 1864.*
I HAVE the honour to acknowledge the receipt of your note of the 8th instant, in regard to the cases of Thomas Tulley and six other men represented to have been improperly enlisted at Portland, Maine. In reply, I have the honour to inform your Lordship that I have called the immediate attention of the Secretary of War to the matter, and have commended your wishes to his favourable consideration.

I have, &c.
(Signed)   WILLIAM H. SEWARD.

Inclosure 3 in No. 15.

Lord Lyons to Mr. Seward.

Sir,   *Washington, May 21, 1864.*
ALTHOUGH only a few hours have elapsed since I informed you in person at the State Department of the grievous intelligence which I had just received respecting some of those Irish passengers by the "Nova Scotian" who were enlisted on their arrival at Portland, I cannot refrain from urging in writing the request which I so earnestly made that measures might be taken without a moment's delay to remove those of them who are still with the army from the danger to which they are hourly exposed.

Since the 19th of March last I have urgently and repeatedly entreated, both verbally and in writing, that these men might not be exposed to meet the enemy in the field, pending the investigation of the lawfulness of their enlistment. No attention has been paid to my request. One of the men, Michael Byrne, has been wounded in the head; another, Edward Cassidy, has also been wounded; a third, Michael Moran, is reported to have been killed. Byrne and Cassidy have been sent to hospitals at Washington. Thomas Burke, James Higgins, and Martin Hogan, if still alive, are no doubt serving with the regiment in which they were enrolled (the 20th Maine Volunteers) in the field.

In the note which I had the honour to receive from you on the 4th instant, I was informed that the cases of these men were in process of investigation, and that a prominent officer implicated in their alleged improper enlistment would be brought to trial. In my answer I expressed my anxiety to be informed that my request that the men had been removed from the theatre of war, and exempted from actual service pending the investigation, had been complied with. I must again urge this often repeated request, and entreat you to move the military authorities to give orders, without a moment's delay, that those of the men who are in hospital may not be sent back to the army, and that those who are in the field may be sent to Washington, or some other place of safety, until the doubts respecting the validity of their enlistment are cleared up.

I have, &c.
(Signed)   LYONS.

Inclosure 4 in No. 15.

Thomas Tulley to Lord Lyons.

Turner's Lane United States' Hospital, Philadelphia,
May 19, 1864.
My Lord,
I TOOK the liberty of informing you on the 5th instant that I was about being sent away from Washington, and as I did not wish to be troubling you with letters, I refrained since from writing; but as I am growing very uneasy I take the liberty, as from the notice I am taking of things I fear I never will be a participator of your goodness unless something is immediately done for me, as they are sending all the men they can to the army. Will your Lordship therefore kindly let me know if there is any chance of my being discharged through your kind influence? As for the other men, I fear something fatal has

H 2

happened them ere this, as the corps they belong to has been in the hottest of the late battles. My people are in want at home, and the Portland authorities have 173 dollars of my bounty which I would like to get, but fearing it would interfere with your Lordship's proceedings, I have not applied for it, although I fear I will not have an opportunity of getting either it or my freedom if something is not shortly done. My people in a great measure depend upon assistance from me, and if your Lordship fails in getting my discharge, perhaps you would get me some Government employ by which I could assist them, and arrange so that I would not be sent to the army. I am losing my health daily on account of my uneasy mind at the position I have got into.

Sincerely praying for your Lordship's health and happiness, and hoping you will condescend to notify to me how matters stand, I have, &c.

(Signed)   THOMAS TULLEY.

P.S.—The doctor here to whom I have related my unhappy circumstances has condemned the Portland authorities for their conduct, and the doctor at Washington said he would send me a good distance, so that I would not have an oportunity of seeing your Lordship.

T. T.

Inclosure 5 in No. 15.

Lord Lyons to Thomas Tulley.

Sir,   *Washington, May 23,* 1864.

I HAVE received your letter of the 19th instant. I have been informed by the United States' Government that a further investigation respecting the enlistment of yourself and your companions is in progress. I am very sorry to say that my endeavours to get your companions removed from the field before the opening of the campaign were unsuccessful. Michael Byrne was at this Legation the day before yesterday. He had been sent to hospital here with a wound in his head. Edward Cassidy has also been sent to a hospital here; he is wounded, but I trust not seriously.

I cannot recommend you to apply for the remainder of the bounty which would be due to you as a recruit, unless you are prepared to acquiesce in the validity of your enlistment.

If you should at any time have reason to believe that you are about to be sent back to the army, I beg you to let me know as soon as possible.

I will do all I can to obtain your discharge, and will write to you again as soon as I am able to give you any information about it.

I am, &c.

(Signed)   LYONS.

No. 16.

Lord Lyons to Earl Russell.—(*Received June* 12.)

My Lord,   *Washington, May 31,* 1864.

WITH reference to my despatch of the 23rd instant, I have the honour to transmit to your Lordship copies of two notes which I have received from Mr. Seward, respecting Thomas Tulley and the other Irish passengers by the steam-ship "Nova Scotian," who were enlisted in the United States' army at Portland.

Your Lordship will see that orders have at last been given to remove these men to Portland, at a distance from the theatre of war, and to cause the legality of their enlistment to be again investigated there.

I have, &c.

(Signed)   LYONS.

Inclosure 1 in No. 16.

Mr. Seward to Lord Lyons.

My Lord, *Department of State, Washington, May 26, 1864.*
I HAVE the honour to acknowledge the receipt of your note of the 21st instant, in relation to the cases of the Irish passengers by the "Nova Scotian," who were enlisted on their arrival at Portland, and in reply to inform your Lordship that I have invited the immediate attention of the Secretary of War to a copy of your Lordship's note, and have recommended a compliance with the requests contained therein.
I have, &c.
(Signed) WILLIAM H. SEWARD.

Inclosure 2 in No. 16.

Mr. Seward to Lord Lyons.

My Lord, *Washington, May 31, 1864.*
I HAVE the honour to recur to your notes of the 7th, 8th, 22nd, 23rd, and 25th ultimo, and 8th and 21st instant, relative to the cases of Thomas Tulley and six other Irish passengers by the "Nova Scotian," and to inclose, for your Lordship's information, a copy of a letter of the 25th instant from the Secretary of War, stating that the men have been ordered to Portland, Maine, with a view to a reinvestigation as to the legality of their enlistment in the army of the United States.
I have, &c.
(Signed) WILLIAM H. SEWARD.

Inclosure 3 in No. 16.

Mr. Stanton to Mr. Seward.

Sir, *War Department, Washington, May 25, 1864.*
I HAVE the honour to advise you that orders have been given that Thomas Tulley and the six others, British subjects, alleged in the communications of Lord Lyons, submitted by you to this Department, to have been improperly enlisted into the military service of the United States, be sent to Portland, Maine, with instructions that their cases be reinvestigated there, it being the point at which the alleged measures for their improper enlistment are stated to have been inaugurated, and where the proof, if any, to that effect, must exist.
I am, &c.
(Signed) E. STANTON.

No. 17.

Lord Lyons to Earl Russell.—(Received June 20.)

My Lord, *Washington, June 6, 1864.*
WITH reference to my despatch of the 31st ultimo, I have the honour to inclose a copy of an order from the War Department, directing that Thomas Tulley, and the other Irish emigrants who were enlisted at Portland shall be sent back to that place in order that a thorough and final investigation of their complaint of having been improperly enlisted may be made.
I have, &c.
(Signed) LYONS.

Inclosure in No. 17.

Special Orders No. 194.

War Department, Adjutant-General's Office,
(Extract.) *Washington, June 2, 1864.*
THE following named enlisted men of Company "D," 20th Maine Volunteers, will upon the receipt of this order at the place where they may be serving, be sent to Captain

Charles H. Doughty, Provost-Marshal, 1st District of Maine, at Portland, Maine, in order that a thorough and final investigation of their complaint of having been improperly enlisted may be made at that city.

The chief mustering offices of the State of Maine will make a full and thorough investigation of this case, and report the result with full particulars to this office.

The depositions of the men themselves will be taken during such investigation.

Privates Thomas Tulley, Michael Byrne, James Higgins, Michael Moran, Edward Cassidy, Thomas Burke, Martin Hogan.

The Quartermaster's Department will furnish the necessary transportation.

By order of the Secretary of War,
(Signed)   E. D. TOWNSEND, *Assistant Adjutant-General.*

No. 18.

Lord Lyons to Earl Russell.—(Received July 2.)

My Lord,   *Washington, June 20, 1864.*

WITH reference to my despatch of the 6th instant, and to my previous despatches respecting the enlistment of Thomas Tulley and the other Irish emigrants who arrived at Portland in the steam-ship "Nova Scotian," I have the honour to transmit to your Lordship copies of further correspondence relative to the fresh investigation of this sad case, which has been ordered by the United States' Government.

There appears to be only too much reason to fear that Thomas Burke and Michael Moran, two of the enlisted men, were killed while serving in the ranks of the United States' army.

I have also the honour to inclose a copy of a note which I have addressed to Mr. Seward in pursuance of the instruction contained in your Lordship's despatch of the 27th ultimo. I have thought it right in this note to act upon your Lordship's instruction without reference to the new investigation which has been ordered, and to urge my request for the discharge of the men on the merits of the case, as it now stands.

I have, &c.
(Signed)   LYONS.

Inclosure 1 in No. 18.

Michael Byrne to Lord Lyons.

My Lord,   *General Hospital, Brattleborough, Vermont, June 7, 1864.*

AS soon as the Doctor understood of me that I had any communication to your Lordship's residence, and that I refused to go from Carver's Hospital, the first opportunity was they sent me away, and did not let me know of it till half an hour before going away, my Lord, so as to prevent me of giving or sending you word of it, so as you might have me retained, until the investigation should be decided upon in our cases at Washington. I would not be let stop in Philadelphia, or in any other place, until I was sent right on to Brattleboro' General Hospital. I also thought I could get to Turner's-lane Hospital at Philadelphia to my comrade, that is, Thomas Tulley, but I could not get any such a chance as that from them. I hope, my Lord, you shall do all in your power for us, and send us word if our cases was investigated into as yet, for before I would go to my regiment again, I would put an end to my life, because I did not 'list with my consent; if I had done so, why I should be as good as any other man, and as I did not, why I shall disobey all orders they give me, for the time to come, and if through my disobedience that it shall be the cause of me to be brought before a Court-martial, there and then I shall call them nothing but a set of murderers for to go send over to my country agents to snap up a lot of men from their wives and families by way of a good employment in Boston, and then as soon as we landed in Portland, to have another lot of agents there to bring us to beer-shops and to drug us, and entrap us to enlist for their armies; but, my Lord, if death is my fate at their hands, my comrades shall let my country know of it, and the whole of what it was for, and also the Government of England, the banners I have fought under in India and other places, that they and my countrymen shall seek for satisfaction for my blood, and strike the iron whilst it is hot, and also I do well know that France would join in it. I shall not speak no more at present.

(Signed)   MICHAEL BYRNE,

D Company, 20th Regiment, Maine Volunteers.

P.S.—I shall expect a speedy answer at your leisure.   Please not to put my regiment nor company in your letters to me.

Inclosure 2 in No. 18.

Lord Lyons to Consul Murray.

Sir,   *Washington, June* 10, 1864.

WITH reference to your despatch of the 7th of April last, and to the previous correspondence relative to the enlistment of Thomas Tulley and six other Irish immigrants in the United States' army, I transmit to you a copy of an order from the War Department, directing that these men be sent to Portland, and that a full and thorough investigation of the case be made. This order has been communicated to me by the Secretary of State of the United States.

You will endeavour to be informed as soon as possible after it takes place of the arrival of any of these men at Portland, and you will put yourself into communication with them, and give them all the advice and assistance you properly can. You will let me know as soon as the men arrive, and you will make reports to me of the nature and progress of the investigation of their case, and keep me informed generally of everything of interest and importance concerning them.

I am, &c.

(Signed)   LYONS.

Inclosure 3 in No. 18.

Lord Lyons to Michael Byrne, &c.

Gentlemen,   *Washington, June* 10, 1864.

I INCLOSE a copy of an order from the War Department, directing that you and the six men enlisted with you shall be sent to Portland in order that a full and thorough investigation of your cases may be made there. The order has been communicated to me by the Secretary of State of the United States.

I conclude that in conformity with the terms of it you will be sent to Portland directly, and I beg you to let Her Majesty's Consul there know of your arrival there as soon as possible after it takes place. I have written to him to ask him to look out for you.

I am, &c.

(Signed)   LYONS.

Inclosure 4 in No. 18.

Consul Murray to Lord Lyons.

My Lord,   *Portland, June* 8, 1864.

I HAVE the honour to transmit herewith a copy of a printed special order, dated the 2nd instant, issued by order of the Secretary of War at Washington, directing that a thorough and final investigation be made by the Provost Marshal at Portland, of the complaint of the seven Irishmen who were enlisted into the 20th Regiment of the Maine Volunteers in March last. A report upon the same formed the subject of my despatch of the 7th of April last.

The chief mustering officer of the State of Maine, Major Gardiner, is to send a Report to the War Department, and the men in question are to be sent to Portland to have their depositions taken.

Of the seven men, Moran and Burke, I understand, were killed at the commencement of the campaign. Byrne and Cassidy were wounded and are in hospital at Washington. Tulley, I hear, did not go on with his regiment, but went to a hospital at Washington; and Higgins and Hogan are the only two left with their regiment.

As I presume I shall also be requested to attend the office of the Provost-Marshal during the second investigation, may I request your Lordship the propriety of my being authorized to employ the services of a lawyer on behalf of these men? The assessor of the Provost Marshal here is a lawyer, and will conduct the case for the Government, and it appears to me that unless the services of a person accustomed to receive and take evidence in these Courts are obtained, the men might be under a considerable disadvantage.

I am still without further information from the office of the Acting Assistant Provost-Marshal General at Augusta regarding the man Collins, although I have written several letters on the subject, and forwarded fresh evidence of Collins' identity which I received from a Mr. James Murray of Nova Scotia.

I have, &c.

(Signed)   H. J. MURRAY.

Inclosure 5 in No. 18.

Lord Lyons to Consul Murray.

Sir,   *Washington, June* 11, 1864.

I HAVE received this morning your despatch of the 8th instant.

Having written to you yesterday on the order to remove Thomas Tulley and six other Irishman, enlisted at the same time, to Portland, I have only to add, that, in conformity with your suggestion, I authorize you to employ a lawyer on behalf of these men, if it shall be in your opinion proper and advisable to do so.

Tulley was, when I last heard from him, in the United States' army hospital, Turner's Lane, Philadelphia, and Michael Byrne at the general hospital, Brattleboro', Vermont. I wrote to them to those places yesterday to inform them of the order, and to recommend them to apply to you as soon as they arrived at Portland. I also wrote a letter in the same sense to the other men, directed to the regiment, although I was not without serious apprehension that they might not all be alive to receive it. I am extremely anxious to receive authentic intelligence of the present condition of each of the seven men.

I am, &c.

(Signed)   LYONS.

Inclosure 6 in No. 18.

Consul Murray to Lord Lyons.

My Lord,   *Portland, June* 15, 1864.

I HAVE the honour to acknowledge the receipt of your Lordship's despatch of the 10th instant, on the subject of the intended re-investigation of the case of Thomas Tulley and the other Irish immigrants who were enlisted into the 20th Maine Regiment in March last. I will faithfully attend to your Lordship's instructions in this affair.

Michael Byrne, who was removed so the General Hospital at Brattleboro', Vermont, arrived here last night on his way to Augusta with a squad of Maine invalids, but had received no orders regarding this case. He told me that Cassidy was on furlough at Boston, and would be difficult to be met with; that Tulley was at Turner's Lane Hospital at Philadelphia with erysipelas; that Burke and Moran being killed, Higgins and Hogan were the only men now with their regiment, if no accident had happened to them.

I have, &c.

(Signed)   H. J. MURRAY.

Inclosure 7 in No. 18.

Lord Lyons to Mr. Seward.

Sir,   *Washington, June* 10, 1854.

HER Majesty's Government have considered the Report made by the Provost Marshal and Board of Enrolment, at Portland, on the case of Thomas Tulley, and the other six Irish immigrants who were enlisted at that place for service in the United States' Army, as well as the reports of Her Majesty's Consul on the same subject.

It appears to Her Majesty's Government that no doubt can be entertained that the enlistment of these Irishmen was the result of a fraudulent scheme contrived and executed in disregard of the laws and neutral rights of Great Britain.

Her Majesty's Government consider that these men were induced in evident bad faith and under false pretences to leave their own country for the purpose of obtaining employment, which was not really ready for them on their arrival in the United States; that on landing at Portland they were designedly plied with drink, and that they were then dealt with in a manner which (although it might be the legal consequence of their disordered condition) made it natural and almost inevitable that they should easily yield to the persuasions of the recruiting agents who were on the look-out for them, and who obtained access to them while they were in confinement, by the aid of the police authorities.

Her Majesty's Government are accordingly of opinion, that notwithstanding the report of the Provost Marshal and Board of Enrolment, they are bound to press their application to the United States' Government for the discharge of these men.

It appears to Her Majesty's Government that as between one Government and another, the testimony of Berwick and Bradley, annexed to the report, of itself suffices to warrant this application. The latter proves that some person (name unknown) carried a large quantity of whiskey to the wharf where the ship lay with the emigrants, and Her Majesty's Government think that it is clear that this person must have been concerned for the recruiting agents, whether those agents directly sanctioned the particular act or not. The former proves that at the liquor store there were "well dressed men" who were "liberal with their money," not drinking themselves, but supplying drink to the unfortunate Irishmen, and who requested the police to aid them in enlisting the Irishmen and giving them drink. Her Majesty's Government consider that upon this evidence and upon the general circumstances of the case, they may reasonably expect to obtain the release of these men; and it is accordingly my duty to renew the request for their discharge from the United States' army, which I made by command of Her Majesty's Government, in the note which I had the honour to address to you on the 23rd April last.

I have, &c.

(Signed)   LYONS.

No. 19.

Lord Lyons to Earl Russell.—(Received July 2.)

My Lord,   *Washington, June 20, 1864.*

I SPOKE to Mr. Seward on the 16th instant in the sense of your Lordship's despatch of the 19th May, respecting the imprisonment of British subjects captured on board neutral vessels, and the practice of drugging men and entrapping them into the United States' naval and military service.

I said to Mr. Seward that your Lordship had desired me to impress on him in friendly communication the duty of putting an end to the imprisonment of British subjects, whose sole offence consisted in their having been on board vessels which had attempted to run the blockade. I added that your Lordship had directed me to point out to him, that while the Government of Great Britain performed its obligations as a neutral to a belligerent, the Government of the United States was bound to perform its corresponding obligations as a belligerent towards a neutral.

I went on to speak of the numerous complaints which had been made to me by British subjects who represented that they had been drugged and enlisted, while not in a state to act for themselves, in the army or navy of the United States. Your Lordship had, I said, been unable to refrain from observing that this practice of drugging men in order to procure their service in the United States' army and navy, was an abuse of the most odious description, and that in the case of the British subjects in question, it justified the strongest remonstrance. But (I added) your Lordship trusted that Mr. Seward, unwilling to excite feelings of just indignation in England, would take measures to put an end to both the abuses, to which I had thus, in obedience to your Lordship's orders, called his attention.

Mr. Seward said that he hoped the recent order of the Secretary of the Navy* would suffice to put an end to all complaints respecting the imprisonment of British subjects captured on board neutral vessels.

With regard to the allegations that men were enlisted while under the influence of drugs or liquors, Mr. Seward said that it was not in the United States alone that such practices were resorted to by unscrupulous recruiting agents; that the complaints made were very much exaggerated, and in many instances entirely unfounded; that at all events he had reason to hope that a check had been given to these practices, and that we should hear very little more of them.

I have, &c.

(Signed) LYONS.

No. 20.

Earl Russell to Lord Lyons.

My Lord,   *Foreign Office, July 6, 1864.*

HER Majesty's Government approve your Lordship's proceedings as reported in your despatches of the 20th ultimo, with reference to the case of Thomas Tulley and the other Irish immigrants, enlisted at Portland and Boston for the United States' military service.

I am, &c.

(Signed) RUSSELL.

---

* *Mr. Welles to Rear-Admiral Farragut.*

Sir,   *Navy Department, May 9, 1864.*

THE following instructions will hereafter be observed with regard to the disposition of persons found on board vessels seized for breach of blockade :—

1. *Bonâ fide* foreign subjects captured in neutral vessels, whether passengers, officers, or crew, cannot be treated as prisoners of war, unless guilty of belligerent acts, but are entitled to immediate release ; such as are required as witnesses may be detained for that purpose, and when their testimony is secured they must be unconditionally released.

2. Foreign subjects captured in vessels without papers or colours, or those sailing under the protection and flag of the insurgent Government, or employed in the service of that Government, are subject to treatment as prisoners of war, and if in the capacity of officers or crew are to be detained. If they are passengers only, and have no interest in the vessel or cargo, and are in no way connected with the insurgent Government, they may be released.

3. Citizens of the United States captured either in neutral or rebel vessels are always to be detained, with the following exceptions :—If they are passengers only, have no interest in vessel or cargo, have not been active in the rebellion, or engaged in supplying the insurgents with munitions of war, &c., and are loyally disposed, they may be released on taking the oath of allegiance. The same privilege may be allowed to any of the crew that are not seafaring men, of like antecedents, and who are loyally disposed.

4. *Pilots and Seafaring Men*, excepting bonâ fide foreign subjects, captured in neutral vessels, are always to be detained. These are the principal instruments in maintaining the system of violating the blockade, and it is important to hold them. Persons habitually engaged in violating the blockade, although they may not be serving on board the vessels, are of this class, and are to be likewise detained.

5. When there is reason to doubt that those who claim to be foreign subjects are in reality such, they will be required to state under oath that they have never been naturalized in this country, have never exercised the privileges of a citizen thereof, by voting or otherwise, and have never been in the pay or employment of the insurgent or so-called "Confederate Government;" on their making such statement they may be released, provided you have not evidence of their having sworn falsely. The examination in case they are doubtful, should be rigid.

6. When the neutrality of a vessel is doubtful, or when a vessel claiming to be neutral is believed to be engaged in transporting supplies and munitions of war for the insurgent Government, foreign subjects captured in such vessels may be detained until the neutrality of the vessel is satisfactorily established. It is not advisable to detain such persons under this instruction, unless there is good ground for doubting the neutrality of the vessel.

7. Parties who may be detained under the foregoing instructions are to be sent to a northern port for safe custody, unless there is a suitable place for keeping them within the limits of your command, and the Department furnished with a memorandum in their cases respectively.

Very respectfully, &c.

(Signed) GIDEON WELLES, *Secretary of the Navy.*

3. Correspondence respecting the Enlistment of Her Majesty's Canadian Subjects in the United States' Army.

No. 1.

Lord Lyons to Earl Russell.—(Received December 26.)

My Lord,   *Washington, December 15, 1863.*

I HAVE the honour to transmit to your Lordship copies of a despatch from Mr. Lousada, Her Majesty's Consul at Boston, and its inclosure, relating to projects which appear to have been formed by private persons in Massachusetts for obtaining men in Canada for the naval and military service of the United States.

I have also the honour to inclose copies of despatches on the subject which I have written to Mr. Lousada and to the Governor-General of Canada.

I have, &c.
(Signed)   LYONS.

Inclosure 1 in No. 1.

Consul Lousada to Lord Lyons.

My Lord,   *Boston, December 5, 1863.*

I HAVE the honour to report to your Lordship, with view of its being communicated to the Governor-General of Canada, that a person called on me this morning for information as to the liability he should incur in attempting to raise on the Canada borders recruits for the United States' service. He was apparently largely supplied with funds, which he exhibited to me. He made no disguise as to his intentions or purposes, and only wanted to know how far the recruiting law of Canada would touch him and his partners.

On my telling him that it was illegal, and that he would have to bear the consequences, he said that he supposed it was no harm to invite men over the boundary line to have a good time at a farm on this side of it, and that there they would be free to do as they pleased. He also said he presumed there was no hindrance to his hiring Canadians for farm service, and that they need not come over the line to effect that bargain.

From other portions of his conversation, not worth repeating in detail, I am satisfied there is an organization on some large scale for enlisting British subjects in Canada, and, as far as my experience goes, those who are foolish enough to be once enticed over the line on any such pretext will find it pretty hard work to get back again out of the clutches of these recruiting gentry.

The high premium offered for recruits, and the total failure of the voluntary enlistment here, foster these schemes.

Since writing above another person (connected with the press) applied. His note and my observations thereon inclosed.

I have, &c.
(Signed)   FRANCIS LOUSADA.

Inclosure 2 in No. 1.

Mr. Dunbar to Consul Lousada.

Sir,
                                                        Boston, December 5, 1863.

A COMMITTEE of the proprietors of slate quarries in Vermont intend to make an effort this winter to procure quarrymen from Wales, to supply the great deficiency of labour which now exists.

A member of the Committee writes to me to ask if I can obtain a certificate under your Consular seal that aliens not naturalized are not compelled to serve in the armies of the United States, as the apprehension of military service is believed to stand in the way of obtaining a very fair supply of labourers from the Welsh quarries.

Will you please to inform me whether you are willing to give such a certificate, and if so, when I shall call at your office to receive it ?

                                 Very respectfully, &c.
                                 (Signed)   C. F. DUNBAR.

Memorandum.

I saw writer of this same day, and distinctly declined to give any such certificate, on two grounds :—Firstly. That although there was no law holding aliens to military service in the United States, yet, practically, such service was obtained every day, and by means almost amounting to compulsion, and redress was so difficult as to be almost unobtainable. Secondly. I was perfectly aware of the use intended to be made of my certificate, and that " Wales " meant the " Canada borders."

The applicant denied this, but admitted that such use might be made of the document.

                                                                   F. L.

Inclosure 3 in No. 1.

Lord Lyons to Consul Lousada.

Sir,
                                                  Washington, December 8, 1863.

I HAVE received this morning your despatch of the 5th instant concerning plans which appear to have been formed for obtaining men from Canada to serve in the United States' army. I have sent to the Governor-General of Canada copies of your despatch and of its inclosure, as well as of the memorandum which you have endorsed upon the latter ; and I have to instruct you to communicate from time to time to his Excellency either directly or through this Legation, as you may deem best under the circumstances, any further information which you may be able to procure on the subject, and especially any particulars as to names, dates, places, or other matters which may assist the Canadian authorities in detecting the persons engaged in these practices and bringing them to justice.

You will of course address the Governor-General directly in all cases in which it is desirable to save time, and you will simultaneously send to me copies of your communications to his Excellency.

I approve of the course taken by you (as stated in the memorandum on the inclosure) with regard to the application made to you for a certificate as to the enlistment of aliens in the service of the United States.

                                           I am, &c.
                                 (Signed)   LYONS.

Inclosure 4 in No. 1.

Lord Lyons to Viscount Monck.

My Lord,
                                                  Washington, December 8, 1863.

I HAVE the honour to transmit to your Excellency copies of a despatch from Her Majesty's Consul at Boston and its inclosure, which relate to plans formed in Massachusetts for obtaining men from Canada to serve in the United States' army. I inclose also a copy of the answer which I have made to the Consul's despatch.

                                           I have, &c.
                                 (Signed)   LYONS.

No. 2.

Lord Lyons to Earl Russell.—(Received April 26.)

My Lord,   *Washington, April* 11, 1864.

I HAVE the honour, with reference to my despatch of the 15th December last, to transmit to your Lordship a copy of a despatch which I have received from Mr. Lousada, Her Majesty's Consul at Boston, respecting a scheme for engaging persons in Canada and Nova Scotia to come to this country as labourers, the real object of which is (as Mr. Lonsada suspects) to obtain recruits for the United States' army.

I inclose also copies of despatches on the subject which I have addressed to the, Governor-General of Canada, and the Administrators of the Government of Nova Scotia and to Mr. Lousada.

    I have, &c.
    (Signed)   LYONS.

Inclosure 1 in No. 2.

Consul Lousada to Lord Lyons.

My Lord,   *Boston, April* 5, 1864.

I HAVE the honour to report that some parties called at my office this morning, and stated that they were about to hire, in Canada and Nova Scotia, 300 labourers to work at some patent-brick works here, and wanted my certificate that it was a *bond fide* transaction. They feared their agent might be molested if he had not some British official paper to show that his mission was a proper one. I refused to give any such document, and did not disguise from them that it was clear to me this was one of the schemes for recruiting the United States' army, and that I should consider myself culpable if in any way, even indirectly, I aided in deluding the poor men they were going to employ in their alleged patent-brick making.

I venture to suggest that if this were brought to the knowledge of the Provincial Governments, it might be of service, and prevent some of the border people being deluded.

    I have, &c.
    (Signed)   F. LOUSADA.

Inclosure 2 in No. 2.

*Lord Lyons to Viscount Monck:**

My Lord,   *Washington, April* 8, 1864.

I HAVE the honour to transmit to your Excellency a copy of a despatch which I have received from Her Majesty's Consul at Boston, respecting a scheme for engaging persons in Canada and Nova Scotia to come to this country as labourers, the real object of which is (as the Consul believes) to obtain recruits for the United States' army.

    I have, &c.
    (Signed)   LYONS

Inclosure 3 in No. 2.

Lord Lyons to Consul Lousada.

Sir,   *Washington, April* 8, 1864.

I HAVE received to-day your despatch of the 5th instant, respecting a scheme to engage persons in Canada and Nova Scotia to come to the United States, ostensibly as labourers, and I have transmitted copies of it to the Governments of those Provinces.

    I am, &c.
    (Signed)   LYONS.

---

* A similar despatch was addressed to Major-General Doyle.

NORTH AMERICA.

No. 17. (1864.)

Correspondence respecting the Enlistment of British
Subjects in the United States' Army.

Presented to the House of Commons by Command
of Her Majesty, 1864.

NORTH AMERICA.
No. 19.   (1864.)

FURTHER CORRESPONDENCE

RESPECTING THE

ENLISTMENT

OF

BRITISH SUBJECTS

IN THE

UNITED STATES' ARMY.

Presented to both Houses of Parliament by Command of Her Majesty.
1864.

LONDON:
PRINTED BY HARRISON AND SONS.
B

Further Correspondence respecting the Enlistment of British Subjects in the United States' Army.

Lord Lyons to Earl Russell.—(Received July 21.)

My Lord, Washington, July 8, 1864.

I INCLOSE copies of the correspondence respecting Thomas Tulley and the six other Irishmen, enlisted on their arrival at Portland, in the steam-ship, "Nova Scotian," which has taken place since I had the honour to address to your Lordship my despatch of the 20th ultimo.

I have the satisfaction of being able to say that six of the men appear to be for the present in safety. The report made to Mr. Consul Murray, that Michael Moran had been killed has happily proved to be erroneous. I fear, however, that there can be little reason to doubt that the seventh man, Thomas Burke, was in fact killed in action, while serving in the United States' Army. I have requested the United States' authorities to communicate to me all the information which they can obtain respecting his fate.

I regret to say that three of the men represent that they were subjected to hardships and indignities of a most unwarrantable kind, on their way from the army of the Potomac to Portland. I have requested that an investigation may be made, and that if the allegations of the men prove to be well-founded, no time may be lost in calling to account those who are responsible for their ill-treatment.

I have also pointed out that I have received nothing more than a formal acknowledgment of my note of the 10th ultimo, repeating my demand for the discharge of the men, and I have reminded Mr. Seward that I am waiting for the answers of the United States' Government to that demand.

I have moreover addressed to Mr. Seward further inquiries respecting James Traynor, the Irish passenger by the "Nova Scotian," who was enlisted at Boston. I have the honour to inclose a copy of my note, and a copy of a note from Mr. Seward acknowledging the receipt of it.

I have, &c.
(Signed) LYONS.

Inclosure 1.

Mr. Seward to Lord Lyons.

My Lord, Department of State, Washington, June 18, 1864.

I HAVE the honour to acknowledge the receipt of your note of the 10th instant, relative to the cases of Thomas Tulley and six other Irish passengers, of the steamer "Nova Scotian," alleged to have being improperly enlisted at Portland, and in reply to inform your Lordship, that I have inclosed a copy thereof, to the Secretary of War, who has the subject under investigation.

I have, &c.
(Signed) WILLIAM H. SEWARD.

Inclosure 2.

Consul Murray to Lord Lyons.

My Lord, *Portland, June 23,* 1864.

I HAVE the honour to acknowledge the receipt of your Lordship's despatch dated the 11th instant, authorizing me to employ a lawyer on behalf of Thomas Tulley and the other Irishmen who were enlisted into the 20th Maine Regiment, if I deem it advisable to do so.

Thomas Tulley presented himself at this office yesterday on his arrival from Philadelphia. He did not appear in uniform, as he stated that he had been deprived of it by two men, who induced him to go and lodge with them at Boston, and who the next morning endeavoured to entice him to re-enlist and accept the bounty money over again. This he refused to do, and came on in the clothes lent him by the master of the house, who he believes was in the plot.

I went with Tulley to the Provost-Marshal, who has sent him to camp Berry, in this immediate neighbourhood, so as to be near at hand when required. Tulley knew nothing about his companions.

Michael Byrne returned from the hospital at Augusta a few days ago, and told me that he had obtained a ten days' furlough. He seemed to have recovered from the wound in the head, but told me that he was suffering from other bodily ailments.

Tulley also acquainted me that he was suffering from a heart disease, and that the sight of his right eye was quite defective.

I have, &c.
(Signed) H. J. MURRAY.

Inclosure 3.

Consul Murray to Lord Lyons.

My Lord, *Portland, June 30,* 1864.

I WENT over to Camp Berry yesterday afternoon to see Thomas Tulley, who had not called upon me since his first arrival, and he told me that Moran, who I understood had been killed, Hogan, and Higgins had arrived at the camp on the previous day, Tuesday. He brought them out to me, and I had some conversation with them. Moran told me that he had been separated from his regiment during action, and was thus reported killed. Both Higgins and Moran seemed in perfect health, but Hogan appeared delicate. They all complained of their treatment during part of their journey to Portland, having been placed in irons and lodged in prison. I have requested them to make a written statement of their cases, which I will forward to your Lordship. The Provost-Marshal here says he knows nothing about it, and concludes that they must have done something wrong to have received this treatment.

Cassidy has not arrived from Boston, and Byrne I have not seen here since his arrival from Cape Fry at Augusta, on a ten days' furlough, as reported to your Lordship in my despatch of the 23rd instant.

I have, &c.
(Signed) H. J. MURRAY.

Inclosure 4.

Consul Murray to Lord Lyons.

My Lord, *Portland, July* 1, 1864.

I HAVE the honour to transmit herewith an original letter which I received yesterday from T. Tulley at Camp Berry, relating, on their behalf, the treatment alleged to have been received by the three Irishmen, Michael Moran, James Higgins, and Martin Hogan, on their journey from the army to Portland, where they were ordered to come in pursuance of a Special Order, No. 194, dated at the War Department, Washington, June 2nd.

This alleged treatment appears so strange and uncalled-for that I can only presume there must have been some misunderstanding of their cases upon the part of the military authorities who forwarded the men on, or that some unacknowledged conduct on their part led to it.

The Provost-Marshal told me to-day that the men arrived from Washington in care of a sergeant, who gave them into his charge, but not as prisoners. The sergeant has returned, and nothing had come to his (Captain Doughty's) knowledge of their alleged ill-treatment or of their misconduct to induce it.

The sergeant's name is believed to be Crook, and he belongs to the Veteran Reserve Corps.

I have, &c.

(Signed)   H. J. MURRAY.

Inclosure 5.

Thomas Tulley to Consul Murray.

Sir,   *Camp Berry, Portland, June 30,* 1864.

I BEG most respectfully to inform you that Michael Moran (reported killed, but still alive), James Higgins, and Martin Hogan, arrived at this camp from the army on the evening of the 28th instant, and I think it right for me to make known to you the treatment they received on their journey. On the receipt of the order from the Secretary at War they were, on the 9th instant, sent from their regiment to the Provost-Marshal's head-quarters, who read and kept the order, and then ordered the men to be placed in the Bull Ring, an open space in the fields, surrounded by armed men, wherein are placed prisoners of all grades. On the next day there was a number of armed men going to Washington, and the above-named sent a note to the Provost-Marshal, explaining their position, and requesting to be forwarded with them, but the captain of the guard made answer that they were not going to puff General Partrick with notes; they were consequently transferred from one Bull Ring to another, from the 9th to the 23rd instant, where they were well nigh starved, as they had at one time to march three successive days without a mouthful of food, and consequently were reduced to eating clover and green apples to support nature. They remonstrated with the authorities, stating that they were not prisoners, but the invariable answer was, they could not be assisted otherwise, as in fact there were in the Bull Ring men dying of hunger, and brought-to in hospital afterwards. On an inspection by the doctor, one of your clients being well nigh dead of hunger, was seen by him, and after making inquiries respecting him and the others, he was informed they were not prisoners but foreigners proceeding to Portland under British protection. The doctor then departed, with apparent disgust, and gave no assistance; and from the feeling of the men, and their conversation of such undeserved and destroying treatment, I firmly allege that no idea can be had of the misery they endured.

On the 23rd they were sent with convicts under guard to Washington, and then transferred to the Old Capitol; from thence they were sent in irons to Boston, where they were left handcuffed together all night, but for the purpose of getting sleep they had to break the cuffs. The consequence was that they were marched through Boston tied with ropes, and arrived in Portland, as before stated. They did their utmost to see Her Majesty's Minister in Washington, but failed, nor could they see you on their arrival, as they were sent under guard to this place.

You have in the foregoing an outline of their travels, but the men say that as long as they live they will not forget the treatment they received, after fighting bravely in all the late battles, as documents from their officers can make manifest.

I hope you will pardon this long letter, but from the kindness we have received from Her Britannic Majesty's Minister and yourself, I thought it incumbent on me to supply you such information, and therefore I have, &c.

(Signed)   THOMAS TULLEY.

Inclosure 6.

Lord Lyons to Mr. Seward.

Sir,   *Washington, July* 7, 1864.

ON the 10th of last month I had the honour to address to you a note, in which, by command of Her Majesty's Government, I renewed the application, which I had made in their name on the 23rd of the previous month of May, for the discharge from the United States' army of the seven Irish passengers by the steam-ship "Nova Scotian," who were enlisted immediately after their arrival at Portland on the 18th of last month. You were so good as to inform me that you had referred my note to the Secretary of War. I await the answer of the United States' Government to the application which it contained. I must in the meantime ask your serious attention to the inclosed copy of a letter addressed to Her Majesty's Consul at Portland on behalf of three of these Irishmen; namely, Michael Moran, James Higgins, and Martin Hogan. I do not doubt that you will cause an investigation to be made of the allegations respecting the hardships and indignities suffered by Moran, Higgins, and Hogan on their way from the army of the Potomac to Portland; and I trust that if these allegations prove to be well founded, no time will be lost in calling to account those who are responsible for the ill-treatment of these unfortunate men.

These three men appear to be now at Portland. I am informed also that Thomas Tulley is at that place, and that Michael Byrne and Edward Cassidy have been removed from the seat of war. The seventh man, Thomas Burke, is reported to have been killed in action while serving in the 20th Regiment of Maine Volunteers. I beg you to be so good as to communicate to me any information respecting his fate which the United States' authorities may be able to obtain.

I have, &c.
(Signed)   LYONS.

Inclosure 7.

Lord Lyons to Consul Murray.

Sir,   *Washington, July 7,* 1864.
I HAVE received your despatches of the 6th, 23rd, and 30th ultimo and 1st instant, relative to the case of Thomas Tulley and the six other Irish passengers by the "Nova Scotian," who were enlisted at Portland.

I have addressed to the Secretary of State of the United States a representation on the subject of the hardships and indignities which three of these men are stated to have suffered on their way from the army of the Potomac to Portland.

I have, &c.
(Signed)   LYONS.

Inclosure 8.

Lord Lyons to Mr. Seward.

Sir,   *Washington, June* 10, 1864.
IN a note which I had the honour to address to you on the 27th of April last, I submitted to you a copy of a despatch from Her Majesty's Consul at Boston, reporting a statement made by James Traynor, one of the Irishmen brought over to Portland by the "Nova Scotian," respecting the circumstances under which he enlisted in the United States' military service. In a note dated the 30th of April you were so good as to inform me that you had referred the matter to the War Department.

I shall be much obliged if you will let me know whether any progress has been made in the investigation of the case.

I have, &c.
(Signed)   LYONS.

Inclosure 9.

Mr. Seward to Lord Lyons.

My Lord,   *Department of State, Washington, June* 20, 1864.
I HAVE the honour to acknowledge the receipt of your note of the 10th instant, inquiring as to the progress of the investigation in the case of James Traynor, one of the Irish passengers of the Steamer "Nova Scotian," alleged to have been improperly enlisted.

In reply, I have the honour to inform your Lordship that I have called upon the Secretary of War for information.

I have, &c.
(Signed)   WILLIAM H. SEWARD.

www.ingramcontent.com/pod-product-compliance
Lightning Source LLC
Chambersburg PA
CBHW022017080426
42733CB00007B/634